Colorado's Colorful Characters

Gladys R. Bueler

PRUETT **P** PUBLISHING COMPANY
Boulder, Colorado

FOREWORD

History is people—people moving in and out of the historical scene—each personality an interesting and colorful study. The vignettes presented here are an introduction to the men and women who wove the fabric of Colorado history. They brought varied backgrounds, talents, and resources; and they played many parts in the mining, industrial, commercial, and political life of the developing state.

Inevitably, myth and legend grow up around such fascinating individuals. Historians find conflicting data: more than one way of spelling a name; differing dates and places; varying interpretations of events and incidents. Often it is a matter of author's choice.

This little book takes both a chronological and a geographical approach. For instance, Chapter II, "PAYDIRT," follows the prospectors up Clear Creek Canyon to Central City, where the exciting mining era began in 1858; Chapter III takes them across the mountains to Leadville and Aspen; finally into the San Juans, presenting in each locale the most interesting personalities. Cripple Creek, the biggest gold camp of them all, was not discovered until 1891, and the people who figured most notably there are presented in Chapter VI.

The Chronology which follows the Vignettes is expanded far beyond the usual listing of dates and events. Between the Chronology and the text, the reader will meet practically every person who had an impact on Colorado and whose name he will hear or read as he travels through the state or delves into its history.

These sketches of Colorado's colorful characters are molded from nuggets extracted from rich veins of historical information that assay high in interest. The mother lode is there in the libraries for those who wish to dig deeper, to cultivate their acquaintance with these unusual individuals and the events that they motivated—or were motivated by.

Gladys Bueler

TABLE OF CONTENTS

TABLE OF CONTENTS (Continued)

Sketch of the Pike Party, in 1806, when they first viewed the Rocky Mountains, coming up from the prairies.

I.

WESTWARD HO!

THE EXPLORERS

"........and called them (the Plains)

........'The Great American Desert'"

In 1803, Napoleon, being hard up for funds, sold France's American lands to the young United States government for $15,000,000, less than 3¢ an acre. In one stroke, the U.S. doubled its size. Curious to find out what it had bought, the government in 1804 dispatched Meriwether Lewis and William Clark to explore the northern section, and in 1806 Lt. Zebulon Montgomery Pike was sent to the southwest, primarily to discover the source of the Red River, the boundary between the newly-acquired lands and Spanish territory.

On July 15, 1806, the young lieutenant (he was only 27) and his party set out from St. Louis. His first mission was to escort 59 Osage Indians safely to their tribe. Eight chiefs had been visiting the Great White Father in Washington; the others had been ransomed by the government after having been captured by another tribe. A month and 500 miles later the rendezvous of the Indians with their families took place. Pike's route so far had followed the Missouri and Osage Rivers; now, freed from his unwieldy party of Indians, he and his official party of 22 headed west, then south, arriving at the Arkansas River in mid-Kansas two months later.

Pike kept a detailed journal, noting the events and sights of each day and the distance traveled. On November 15, he makes the first mention of the mountain that now bears his name, Pikes Peak. He writes, "At two o'clock in the afternoon I thought I could distinguish a mountain to our right, which appeared like a small blue cloud; viewed it with the spy-glass, and was still more confirmed in my conjecture . . . in half an hour, they appeared in full view before us. . . . Killed three buffalo. Distance 24 miles." Several times between the 15th and 27th of November he makes such comments as, "Marched at our usual hour, pushed with an idea of arriving at the mountains, but found at night no visible

1

difference in their appearance from what we did yesterday." Anyone who has headed toward the mountains has been baffled by the gap between their seeming closeness and their actual distance away. Pike was no exception. (In fact, as far back as the 1870s, a joke was going the rounds about a party coming to an irrigation ditch as they approached the mountains. To the surprise of the others, one man started stripping to his underwear. "What in the world are you doing?" the others wanted to know. "You can step over this ditch." "I've been fooled once too often," answered the hiker. "I'm going to swim this d - - - - - d river.")

By November 27th Pike's "Grand Peak" still "appeared at the distance of 15 or 16 miles from us." At this point Pike made an oft-quoted statement, one that is almost surely misinterpreted: ". . . it would have taken a whole day's march to arrive at its base, when I believe no human being could have ascended to its pinical (sic)." Without question this statement referred to his own group, whose provisions were low and whose clothing was light, and not to future generations. (Actually, of course, the pinical of Pikes Peak has been reached by more people than any other mountain in the world except Fujiyama in Japan. They have ascended by foot, burro, carriage, cog train, automobile.)

Z. M. Pike

By December 2, when Pike resumed his westward journey, the thermometer stood at 2° below zero and his men were beginning to suffer from frozen feet. They killed two buffalo bulls, "that the men might use pieces of their hides for mockinsons (sic). . . . Killed six turkeys. Distance 20 miles."

Pike's report now contains the first mention of the gorge later called "Royal," a spectacular gash in the earth's crust through which runs the Arkansas River. They "followed the river into the mountain," but finding the going too rough, climbed to the rim to continue on across South Park to the Arkansas—which they were sure was the Red. Near Buena Vista they spent Christmas day, 1806. Pike describes it: "The hardships and privations we underwent were on this day brought more fully to our mind. . . . Here 800 miles from the frontiers of our country, in the most inclement season of the year; not one person clothed for the winter, many without blankets (having been obliged to cut them up for socks, etc.) and now laying down at night on the snow or wet ground; one side burning whilst the other was pierced with the cold wind. . . . I will not speak of diet, as I conceive that to be beneath the serious consideration of a man on a voyage of such nature." While he "will not speak of diet" on Christmas day, he mentioned on Christmas Eve that "all the refreshment we had to celebrate that day with, was buffalo meat, without salt, or any other thing whatever."

They followed the frozen river downstream, still thinking it was the

2

Red. Pike divided his little party into small groups and "every one had to depend on his own exertion for safety and subsistance (sic)." They came to a deep, steep gorge; and after fighting their way through it, Pike, to his amazement looked out on "the unbounded space of the prairies. . . . I immediately recognized it to be the outlet of the Arkansaw (sic), which we had left nearly one month since! This was a great mortification. . . . This was my birth-day, and most fervently did I hope never to pass another so miserably. Distance 7 miles." (This was January 5, 1807, Pike's 28th birthday.)

By January 9, the stragglers had caught up, and the party was together —right back where they had started on December 10th (near the State Pen at Canon City). They "felt comparatively happy, notwithstanding the great mortifications I experienced at having been so egregiously deceived as to the Red River." Pike decided to build a small stockade and leave part of the baggage and two men, the rest to carry the necessary Indian presents, ammunition, tools, etc. on their backs, and turn south. The packs averaged 70 pounds each.

They marched on the 14th; and on the 17th "when we halted . . . for encampment . . . we discovered that the feet of nine of our men were frozen." Even so, they had made 28 miles that day. The next day Pike and Dr. Robinson went out "to hunt something to preserve existence." They wounded a buffalo, "but had the mortification to see him run off notwithstanding. We concluded it was useless to go home to add to the general gloom and sat up all night . . . hungry and without cover." Home, he says!

Reluctantly leaving the men with the frozen feet behind, the others marched on, sometimes in snows three feet deep. On the 20th two more could go no further and two others could not carry their loads and could only shuffle along with the help of a stick. Pike left the two, with encouragement "to have fortitude to resist their fate. . . . We parted, but not without tears." (Amazingly, all these men were rescued and finally reunited in Santa Fe. During all these travels, the little party was constantly breaking up into scouting groups, hunting parties, etc. Considering the immensity and ruggedness of the land and the many dangers from weather, wild animals, savages, accidents, one of the most remarkable accomplishments of the whole enterprise was that these groups ever found each other.)

They crossed the mountains into the San Luis Valley, and here Pike has another first: The first mention of the Sand Dunes. He thought they looked like "the sea in a storm" except for their color. Thousands of later visitors have had the same impression as they viewed these 1000-foot-high dunes piled up when sands are caught in turbulent wind currents at a low point in the mountains and deposited at their base instead of being carried on over them. The tireless winds constantly shift the loose surface sand into ocean-like waves.

Marching on, the intrepid little group came to a large river—which they were sure was the Red. (It was the Rio Grande; they were near Alamosa.) On the wooded banks of a side stream, the Rio Conejos, Pike decided to build a stockade, "that four or five might defend against the

3

insolence, cupidity and barbarity of the savages, whilst the others returned to assist the poor fellows who were left behind at different points."

On February 16th, Pike and one of his men, while out hunting, "discovered two horsemen. . . . As my orders were to avoid giving alarm or offence to the Spanish government of New Mexico, I endeavored to avoid them at first." After some skirmishing and flourishing of lances, Pike "hollowed to them that we were Americans and friends, which were almost the only two words I knew in the Spanish language. . . . As I knew them to be spies, I thought proper to inform them that I was about to descend the river to Natchitoches." (Nachitoches, Louisiana, is on the Red River, which rises in the Texas Panhandle and flows into the Mississippi about a hundred miles north of New Orleans. The Red was far south and east of the area in which Pike was searching.)

Ten days later 100 Spanish dragoons appeared at the stockade. Pike reports his meeting with Don Ignatio Saltelo, commandant of the party. " 'Sir, the governor of New Mexico being informed you had missed your route, order me to offer you, in his name, mules, horses, money, or whatever you may stand in need of to conduct you to the head of Red River; as from Santa Fe to where it is sometimes navigable, is eight days journey.' 'What?' said I, interrupting him, is not *this* the Red River?' 'No sir, the Rio del Norte,' (Rio Grande)." One can imagine Pike's surprise and chagrin at this astounding news.

The dragoons escorted Pike and his men to Santa Fe (where the others caught up with him), then to Chihuahua, Mexico, finally back to U.S. soil. On July 1, 1807, just two weeks short of a year from the time his adventure began, he reached Natchitoches. He had finally come to the Red.

Pike has been called the "lost pathfinder" because much of the time he didn't know where he was. How could he? There were no guide books to consult—he was writing the first one himself.

* * * * *

Years passed, but knowledge of the west remained vague. It became increasingly urgent that maps be made and the geography of the Louisiana Purchase area be studied. In 1820, Major Stephen H. Long was commissioned to explore the Missouri, Platte, Arkansas, and Red Rivers. His party of 22 included a naturalist and other scientists, Spanish and Indian interpreters, and a landscape painter, Titian Peale. (Peale was the youngest son of Charles Willson Peale, the famous portrait painter of revolutionary days, who named all his sons for Renaissance artists. Titian's older brothers were Raphaelle, Rembrandt, and Rubens. Later, Titian Peale was to have a similar assignment with the same kind of exploratory campaign in Australia.)

The Long expedition set out in June and went up the South Platte. At one point they took their bearings on a high mountain to the West which they assumed to be the grand peak Pike had described. They found out their mistake when they learned that it was another high peak which the French called *Les deux Oreilles* (The Two Ears); today it is named Long's Peak.

Long's party turned south along the Front Range and came to the base of Pikes Peak, where they camped. Dr. Edwin James, a 23-year-old naturalist, and two others made the first recorded ascent of the already famous peak. Pike himself had found his majestic mountain "to be spoken of with admiration by the Spaniards of New Mexico and to be known, as well, to the savage nations." Dr. James was astounded to find clouds of grasshoppers on the summit. On the descent they saw smoke ahead, and realized that the flames of their campfire had spread. The naturalist was much concerned that the smoke might be seen by hostile Indians, but

seemed undisturbed that man's carelessness had started a forest fire. Conservation was an unknown word in 1820. In honor of his feat, Long named the mountain *James Peak*. It was not until Fremont put the name *Pikes Peak* on his maps in 1843 that this name became the permanent designation.

When they reached the Arkansas, Long divided his party. One group, under Captain John Bell, was to continue down the Arkansas. Long himself would continue south to search for the source of the elusive Red River. They came to a river—which they were sure was the Red. For a month they followed it downstream. Then, on September 10, they arrived at its confluence with a much larger waterway and realized they had come to the Arkansas. Since the Red

Stephen H. Long

entered the Mississippi far south of the Arkansas, they reluctantly conceded that the river they had been following could not be the Red. (Actually, it was the Canadian.) So Pike wasn't the only "lost pathfinder." Long never did get over his chagrin at his failure to find the river he was sent to explore. It was 32 years before someone finally went down the Red and knew where he was.

Major Long didn't think much of the plains east of the Rockies, and called them *The Great American Desert*. He gave it as his considered opinion that the whole area was "almost wholly unfit for cultivation" but that it "might serve as a barrier to prevent too great an extension of our population westward." He would be mightily surprised today to see the wonders irrigation has worked, and the explosion of population west of the Mississippi.

Major Long was so busy with map-making that he left it to Dr. James to write the official report of the expedition. It so stirred the imagination of people in the East that it helped bring about that very "extension of our population westward" that Long feared.

Major Long presented a precise accounting of the cost of his expedition to the Secretary of War: $20,348.17½. (The last half-cent piece was minted in 1857.)

THE MOUNTAIN MEN

When Zebulon Pike was taken to Santa Fe by his Spanish captors, he was undoubtedly surprised to be met there by another American, James Purcell. Three years before Pike's expedition in 1806, Purcell had wandered into the mountains while trapping beaver and had been captured by Indians but had escaped and made his way to Santa Fe. He told Pike of finding gold in South Park, but this news received scant attention. Purcell was the first of the intrepid Mountain Men.

In the years between the Pike and Long explorations, many young, hardy, adventurous men came to the mountains to trap beaver. At the time, fashionable men were wearing tall beaver hats, and beaver pelts were at a premium, making trapping a profitable business. The Mountain Men were a hardy breed that added much of valor and excitement to the early days of Colorado. Many of them later became famous as guides and scouts for explorers, emigrant parties, and military campaigns. In 1822 General William Ashley formed the Rocky Mountain Fur Company and hired these rugged individualists to work for him. Before they scattered for spring trapping, Ashley selected a point where all should assemble, or rendezvous, the following July. For 15 years the summer rendezvous was the most colorful feature of the fur trade days. Trappers, who for months had lost themselves in the mountains, enjoyed the holiday riotously. Racing, gambling, drinking were paid for with beaver pelts, as were all sorts of trinkets to delight the heart of the trappers Indian "wife."

William Bent

As beaver hats went out of style, the market for pelts dwindled and had practically disappeared by 1840. But by now, buffalo skins, obtained through trade with the Indians, had become popular for coats, bedding, rugs. Trappers gradually turned to hunting or trading, and trading posts were set up where they could meet the Indians. The first large business enterprise in Colorado was such a post—Bent's Fort, built around 1830 on the Santa Fe Trail between La Junta and Las Animas by William and Charles Bent and a Frenchman, Ceran St. Vrain. For 20 years Bent's Fort was a gathering place and a home away from home for mountain men, soldiers, adventurers.

The trappers and traders brought their "wives" (Mexican or Indian women) and their half-breed children played noisily with the numerous Indian progeny whose parents had pitched their tents around the fort. Clerks worked busily inside, and patrols with loaded muskets walked the battlements. Business was so good by 1838 that a second post was estab-

6

lished, on the South Platte. It was named Fort St. Vrain for the third partner, who was reputed to be a French nobleman.

William Bent, called Little White Man by the Indians because he was just 15 when he came into the territory as an employee of the American Fur Company, married Owl Woman, daughter of White Thunder, a Cheyenne medicine man. She died, and he married her sister, Yellow Woman. His brother Charles married Inezita Jaramillo, sister of Kit Carson's Mexican wife. When Col. Stephen W. Kearney's men "conquered" New Mexico (without firing a shot) in 1846, Charles Bent was appointed the first territorial governor of New Mexico. Some of the Indians and Mexicans were unhappy under the new government and they revolted, charged into Bent's home, assassinated him, and paraded his gray scalp through the streets of Taos.

William Bent continued the business at the Fort for a few years after his brother's death, but trading was becoming less profitable each year and he tried to sell the fort to the government as a military station. Negotiations dragged on so long that finally, in 1849 in disgust he loaded his goods on 20 large wagons and blew up the fort.

* * * * *

In 1809 two baby boys were born not very far apart, one in Illinois, the other in Kentucky. One was to become legend in the east, the other in the west. One was tall, lanky, angular, dark; the other was small, thickset, sandy-haired. Neither would seem to have been likely candidates for lasting fame. One was Abraham Lincoln, the other Christopher Carson. Abe Lincoln was to attain heroic stature by preserving the Nation; Kit Carson was to become the folk hero of its expansion westward.

Kit Carson

When Kit was a year old his family moved to the frontier in Missouri. By the time he was a teen-ager, mountain men with General Ashley's Rocky Mountain Fur Company were swaggering into the little settlement of Franklin, telling breath-taking tales of adventure and danger in the Wild West; prairie schooners creaked and rumbled westward; pack trains laden with beaver pelts and buffalo skins plodded in. Kit and his chums listened open-mouthed and watched bug-eyed.

Kit's father had died when he was nine; his mother struggled to rear him and his 13 brothers and sisters; when he was 16 he was apprenticed to a saddler. A year later, on October 6, 1826, an advertisement appeared in the *Missouri Intelligencer*: "Notice . . . That Christopher Carson, a boy about 16 years old, small of his age, but thickset, light hair, ran away from the subscriber . . . to whom he had been bound to learn the saddler's trade. . . . One cent reward will be given to any person who will

7

bring back the said boy. (Signed) David Workman." The thirst for adventure generated by the sights and sounds of frontier Franklin had made civilization too tame for 17-year-old Kit Carson to endure. Nobody could catch him to claim the one cent reward. Kit had run away to the West to become the most famous of all the Mountain Men.

At the summer rendezvous in 1835, Kit fought a duel with another trapper over an Arapahoe girl, then took her as his "wife." Her name was Waa-nibe, *Grass Singing,* but Kit re-named her Alice. A daughter was born to them, and Kit named her Adeline, for a niece who was his age and who had been his childhood playmate. Later, Kit sent little Adeline back east for schooling. The happy singing of Waa-nibe was stilled when Adeline was but a baby, and lonely Kit "womaned" again, with *Making-Out-The-Road,* a Cheyenne. This alliance didn't turn out too well. Making-Out-The-Road was extravagant, and when Kit remonstrated she drove him out of their lodge at Bent's Fort and flung his belongings after him. He was working as a hunter at the famous trading post, earning $1 a day.

His third wife (but his first marriage) was a beautiful Mexican girl, Josefa Jaramillo, who brought him rich lands as her dowry and who bore him seven children. At the time of their marriage Josefa was 15, Kit 34. It was a very happy marriage; even so, Josefa never quite succeeded in domesticating him.

Most years of his life were spent away from home. He was guide, friend, and trusted courier to Lt. John C. Fremont, The Pathfinder, on the first three of his five government-authorized explorations in the West. Kit made several trips to Washington with official dispatches, and it was he who carried in his saddle-bags the first news of the discovery of gold in California. The official message he delivered to President Polk was written by Lt. William Tecumseh Sherman, later General Sherman of marching-through-Georgia fame. Kit also carried a copy of the *California Star* of April 1, 1848. The exciting news in the message and the paper started the stampede to California, ten years before the gold rush to Colorado.

Kit Carson fought in the Mexican War; the Indian Wars (though he always had great sympathy with and understanding of the Indians); and rendered valuable aid to the Union during the Civil War. He rose from Lieutenant to Brigadier-General of Volunteers. Both before and after the War, Kit held appointment as Indian Agent at Taos, where he and Josefa had their home. He came to believe, by the end of the Civil War, that the only hope for peace as far as the Indians were concerned was to put them in reservations; for he felt that if they continued living as they were, killing the cattle and sheep of the settlers to appease their hunger and work off their thirst for revenge, disastrous confrontations would inevitably result.

In July, 1846, during the Mexican War, Kit was with Fremont at Monterey on the California coast. Fremont and Commodore Robert Stockton planned a joint land and sea action, and Fremont and Kit and the other men were inducted into the *Navy Battalion of Mounted Riflemen.* Mountain Man Kit Carson, sailor in name only, was seasick all the

8

Kit Carson with John C. Fremont, taken in Washington, D.C., when the two were planning one of their Western adventures.

Fort Garland in the San Luis Valley, a command of Kit Carson. Today it is an outstanding example of historic restoration by the Colorado Historical Society.

9

way down to San Diego and vowed if he ever got off that ship he would never travel by any other means than a horse or mule for the rest of his natural life. He didn't.

* * * * *

Mountain Man Jim Bridger was almost, if not quite, as famous as Kit Carson. The two were together on many an exciting occasion. A tall, lank fellow with little refinement and less education, Jim was one of the first young men to join Ashley's Rocky Mountain Fur Company, in 1822. He, too, was a familiar figure at Bent's Fort. He was engaged as guide by Sir George Gore, an Irish nobleman and sportsman who came to Colorado in 1855 with one of the largest hunting parties ever to roam the West. There were secretaries, servants, cooks, dog-tenders, wranglers, hunters; wagons, carts; several span of oxen, strings of horses, packs of dogs. Sir George roughed it with the best of them in his outings, but back at his elaborate base camp he lived like a nobleman. In the evenings he read from Shakespeare to his captive audience, and Jim Bridger, hearing of Falstaff for the first time, said he "calkerlated that that big fat Dutchman Full-Stuff was a leetle too fond of beer."

Sir George and his hunters slaughtered so many animals, including several thousand buffalo, that the Indians began to fear for their food supply and thought seriously of slaughtering the play-boy hunter himself. Sir George Gore left his name forever inscribed on the map of Colorado— in the Gore Range and Gore Creek.

After his guiding days in Colorado and throughout the West, Jim Bridger built Fort Bridger on the Green River in Wyoming, almost as famous a stopping place as Bent's Fort.

* * * * *

Tom Fitzpatrick, fresh from Ireland, read General Ashley's advertisement for young men to join his fur trapping operations in the Rockies (in 1822) and was one of the first to respond. He went on to become one of the most legendary of the famous trappers and guides. Somewhere along the way, he suffered a hand injury which gave him a lasting nickname among the Indians—Broken Hand. (There is a Broken Hand peak in the Sangre de Cristos, near Kit Carson peak.) Like Carson, Broken Hand Fitzpatrick guided Fremont, Kearney, emigrant parties and military campaigns in Colorado and all over the west. Col. Kearney wrote that Fitzpatrick "had as good, if not better, knowledge of the Rockies than any other man in existence."

After the Mexican War the United States government initiated peace negotiations with the Plains Indians, hoping to stop their raiding on the Santa Fe and Oregon Trails, and in 1846 Fitzpatrick was appointed Indian agent for the region of the Platte and Arkansas Rivers. Both Indians and white men acclaimed his appointment.

The era of the trappers, the traders, the trading posts, was over by the mid 1850s. When the '59ers came across the plains in their covered wagons, they found the trading posts in ruins and grass growing on the old trails. But these frontiersmen had been the real trail blazers, the

10

pathfinders, who opened up the west for the later pioneers and settlers.

In 1929 Mrs. Ann Woodbury Hafen wrote a tribute to *Broken Hand, Chief of the Mountain Men* which epitomizes not only the life of one man, Tom Broken Hand Fitzpatrick, but of the entire era of the Mountain Men:

BROKEN HAND,

CHIEF OF THE MOUNTAIN MEN*

Trapper

Young sun-bronzed weathered face . . .
Long wind-tossed hair,
Keen eyes like winter stars . . .
No book reveals the winding of your ways.
But a smoke-etched suit records . . .
The dangers and the doings of your days:
Grease smears of skinning knife,
Dark stains of trickled blood, . . .
Fringe snagged by thorn of brush
Or ripped by grizzly claw.
Knife-cut
Where a challenger at Summer Rendezvous
Hot with bad liquor
Slashed but missed his mark. . . .
Your days, an endless search for beaver sign . . .
Up virgin streams that swallow human scent
You lug steel cunning traps . . .
Spring trapping done, what then?
Like pirate to his chest
You dig from secret cache
Pelt treasures to fur-hat the world!
With stacks of hairy banknotes
Off to Rendezvous where trappers holiday
And barter furs.

Guide

Up table land, on through the mountain gates,
Explorer, soldier, missionary band,
Home-seekers, visioning a sunset land,
Follow your footsteps.
You choose a camp with water, grass, and wood.
You husband the supplies; you ration food.
You bolster courage, reconstruct disaster—
    Guide of the western trail!

11

Indian Agent

Ambassador of peace
Promoter of understanding
You mediate between
The feathered warrior and the rash dragoon . . .
To red men groping through a maze
Of ways disaster-fraught,
You point a path
To bloodless peace!

INDIANS ON THE WARPATH

" Ouray asked, 'Is not the U. S. strong

enough to keep it's treaties ?' "

he "path to bloodless peace" was still years away when, in the early 1860s, the pioneers began streaming across the plains toward the Rockies in their white-topped wagons—through country the Indians considered their own. White men's horses and oxen ate the grass; white hunters killed the buffalo. The mining camps in the mountains, the farms along the streams, the clusters of houses in the burgeoning cities, were crowding the red man from the land of his fathers. He must rise up and fight, or forever lose his heritage!

John M. Chivington

The Plains Indians went on the warpath. Stages were attacked; freight wagons bringing essential supplies were captured or destroyed. Settlements were raided, buildings burned, horses stampeded, cattle stolen, people murdered. In the summer of 1864, when the mutilated bodies of the Hungate family, who lived 30 miles southeast of Denver, were brought into the city and exhibited, the horrified citizens demanded revenge.

In mid-August martial law was declared in Denver, and all male citizens were required to register for some kind of military service. The formation of a regiment of volunteer cavalry for 100 days of service was authorized, and a thousand men enlisted under Col. John M. Chivington, Commander of the Colorado Military District. Chivington, who before his military service had been a Methodist minister and religious leader, set out to train and equip his *hundred-daysers*. Some were farmers and ranchers who had been driven from their homes by Indian raids; some were miners; others, townsmen of many trades. None were trained soldiers. The very Indian raids that helped bring on the crisis kept the supplies necessary to equip the men from arriving. Thirty of the hundred days ticked away.

In the meantime, after much palaver with Governor Evans, the Cheyennes under Black Kettle and the Arapahoes under Left Hand had indicated their willingness to sign a peace treaty. It was a wily move, what with winter coming on. The Indians knew that, so long as they were peacefully encamped, the federal government would keep them in supplies. But stories of atrocities by other bands of Indians continued to come in and Denver citizens became more and more tense.

A second 30 days passed by. People began to call Chivington's Third Regiment the "bloodless Third." It became clear that if the hundred daysers were ever going to fight the Indians, they would have to get to it.

On November 20, with less than a month of service left, the civilians in uniform were ordered to march. A blizzard hit and a few men died and others deserted. The rest just wanted to get the bloody business over and get home. On the 26th, they encamped near the site of Bent's Fort, and on the night of the 28th, they were ordered forward.

On the morning of November 29, Black Kettle was startled to see an army approaching, and hurriedly raised an American flag with a white flag tied beneath it. This did not stop Colonel Chivington—he ordered his men to attack. Guns blazing, the soldiers charged into the camp, slaughtering braves, women, and children indiscriminately. In Colonel Chivington's official report he said, "Between five and six hundred Indians were left dead upon the field . . . making almost an annihilation of the entire tribe." The victorious soldiers carried away a hundred scalps, which were proudly displayed at a Denver theater.

So shocking was the event that a Congressional committee was appointed to study the matter. The committee's 118-page report condemned Colonel Chivington for having "deliberately planned and executed a foul and dastardly massacre which would have disgraced the veriest savage among those who were the victims of his cruelty."

The Sand Creek Massacre was hostly debated for years. Was it a *massacre* of Indians peaceably assembled? Or was it a *battle* in which the Indians got treatment they richly deserved for such atrocities as one witness at the hearings, Major Anthony, described: the dismembering of ten white men, with "the innocent (?) squaws and harmless (?) children" kicking the remains around like balls?

Whichever interpretation is correct, the Sand Creek Massacre has gone down in history as one of Colorado's bloodiest events, and one that Coloradans wish had never happened.

As word of the massacre spread, the Plains Indians, bent on revenge, cut communications, raided settlements, accosted stages and wagon trains, and sacked and burned Julesburg, a major way-station for stagecoaches and freight lines. Martial law was declared in the whole area, and U.S. troops released from Civil War engagements were hurried in from the east. Battles between troops and the Indians were frequent and gory. Finally, in 1867, treaties were made whereby the Plains Indians gave up title to all their territory in Colorado, and were settled on a reservation in Oklahoma.

* * * * *

The Utes had always lived in the splendid and forbidding wilderness they called the *Shining Mountains,* the western slope of the Rockies. In the summers they forayed into the big parks between the mountain ranges or out onto the eastern plains to hunt buffalo. Sometimes they fought battles with the Plains Indians, their traditional enemies. But sometimes they met in peace with them at the place where the spirit of the Great God Manitou lived in the bubbling springs at the base of Pikes Peak. When the white men came, the Utes were not unfriendly.

The Ute nation was made up of several tribes. The great Ouray was chief of one of these, the Uncompahgre. Ouray, the *Arrow,* was born "the year the stars fell," 1833. That year the Leonids, meteors from the constellation Leo, were especially heavy, and those who knew the meaning of the stars said he was born to be a leader. His father was an Uncompahgre Ute, his mother a Jicarilla Apache. However, he was brought up by a Spanish family in Taos, and learned to speak both Spanish and English. When he was 17, Ouray came into his inheritance—several ponies and the leadership of the Uncompahgre tribe.

His unusual upbringing was to make Ouray an invaluable negotiator between the Utes and the Great White Father in Washington. Several times he was sent to Washington as representative of his people, and impressed everyone with his dignity and knowledge. On one occasion he met President Grant and his wife and daughter at the White House and delighted the First Family by calling them Great Father, Great Mother, and Great Sister. At the zoo the Indians saw elephants for the first time, and made up a word for them; translated, it meant "the big high animal with a tail at each end."

In 1868 the United States government negotiated a treaty with the Utes. By its terms the Utes relinquished all claim to lands in the San Luis Valley; and the government generously "gave" them most of the land on the western slope. Since these were their ancestral lands anyway, the Indians were content.

Five years later the Utes were persuaded to sign another treaty establishing boundaries. This, too, they accepted. But after the surveyors had finished and the boundaries were drawn, the Utes found they had lost their best land. It was no happenstance that this particular section was the rich mining area of the San Juans. Prospectors had already begun digging into the earth and removing the ore—an offense, the Indians said, to their gods.

Chief Ouray protested; the Great White Father hedged. Ouray wondered, "Is not the United States government strong enough to keep its treaties?" Strong enough not to, both mountain and plains Indians soon found out.

As soon as the treaty was signed there was a headlong stampede of prospectors into the San Juans and many small mining camps sprang up where, a short time before, teepees had housed braves and their squaws and papooses. Chief Ouray was able to keep his Uncompahgre Utes quiet; but he could not control lesser chiefs, and these and their bands struck terror into the hearts of the miners and their families.

14

An artist's representation, from Harpers Weekly, reporting "The Ute War—Major Thornburgh's Last Charge." Coming to the aid of Meeker, Thornburgh and his troops were ambushed at Milk Creek on Sept. 29, 1879.

A similar sketch showing a representation of death and destruction at the White River Agency, after the Ute raid on Sept. 30, 1879.

15

Company K, 10th Infantry, Capt. Hanson commanding, at Uncompahgre Cantonment, between Montrose and Ouray, Colo., Nov. 5, 1886.

An unidentified group of Ute braves.

Nathan C. Meeker

Especially, trouble brewed in the north with the White River tribe, for whom Nathan C. Meeker was the Agent. Before 1870 Mr. Meeker had been the agricultural editor of Horace Greeley's New York Tribune. In 1859 Greeley had visited the Colorado mining camps and advised "Go West, young man"; now he sent Meeker with 50 families to found the Union Colony on the Cache la Poudre River, and they named the settlement Greeley. Eight years later, his colonization activities successfully completed, Meeker, now 60, became the Indian Agent at White River. Here was a challenge he had long dreamed of. He had a theory on the Indian problem, a plan for the Indians something like the Greeley colony. It would be a way for the Indians to by-pass several centuries, to make, quickly and easily, the transition from the nomad life of the hunter to the settled life of the farmer. Unfortunately, Meeker failed completely to understand the Indian and his ways.

He insisted the Utes abandon their teepees and live in houses, become farmers and till the fields, send their children to the school which his daughter Josephine set up, become Christians with the help of the "Spirit Book" Mrs. Meeker lived by. The more insistent Meeker became, the more resistant became the Indians. Finally he determined to plow up the pasture where the Utes kept their ponies and ran their races, and force them to plant a crop there. This was the final straw for the Indians.

On September 30, 1879, they stormed the agency, stole the guns and goods, set fire to the buildings, killed and mutilated Meeker, massacred his ten employees, and took Mrs. Meeker, Josephine, and another woman and two children as hostages.

The Meeker Massacre further enraged the people of Colorado and they demanded drastic measures against the Utes. Six months later Congress made its decision: The Utes must go. They must be removed to reservations in Utah. (The Utes pronounced their name *Yoo-tah*, hence the name of the Territory, later the State, of Utah.) Each Ute was to receive his per capita share of an annual annuity of $50,000. As he made his mark on the treaty, one chief remarked sadly that it was the best the Utes could do.

In September, 1881, nearly 1,500 Utes, driving ahead of them 10,000 sheep and goats, riding or herding 8,000 ponies, began the weary 13-day march to their new home in the arid lands of Utah. Captain James Parker of the Fourth Cavalry described the pitiful sight. "The whole Ute nation on horseback and on foot was streaming by . . . women and children were loudly wailing. . . . It was inevitable that they should move, and better then than after a fruitless and bloody struggle. . . . The soldiers marched behind, pushing the Indians out, and the whites hurried in be-

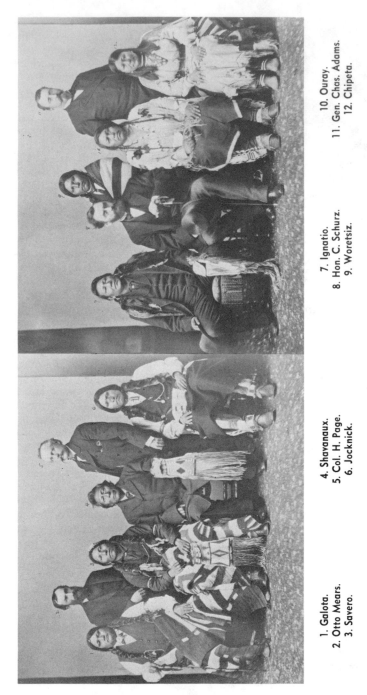

1. Galota.
2. Otto Mears.
3. Savero.

4. Shavanaux.
5. Col. H. Page.
6. Jocknick.

7. Ignatio.
8. Hon. C. Schurz.
9. Woretsiz.

10. Ouray.
11. Gen. Chas. Adams.
12. Chipeta.

13. Oho Blanco.
14. Wm. H. Berry.
15. Tapuch

16. Capt. Jack.
17. Tim Johnson.

18. Sowerwick.
19. Henry Jim.
20. Buckskin Charley.

21. Wass.
22. Wm. Burns.
23. Alhandra.

Photographed in Washington, D.C., after the signing of the 1873 San Juan Treaty (2nd). As a special inducement and to show the Indians the futility of resistance, the government sent the group to the East, accompanied by Otto Mears, who interpreted. This was the treaty that opened the San Juan's to the miners.

19

hind the soldiers, taking up the land. In three days the rich lands of the Uncompahgre were occupied, towns were being laid out, and lots being sold at high prices."

Chipeta, *White Singing Bird,* Ouray's wife, went with her people into exile on the reservation. But Chief Ouray stayed in the Great Mountains as he had always said he would—he had died a year before. He had become ill a short time after the signing of the final treaty. The Americans sent their doctors, but he would not see them. He made a sign and the medicine men of his tribe came and sang to him for many days. One day he raised up and said in a strong voice, "Ouray will never leave the Shining Mountains." Then he closed his eyes and his spirit went to join those of his ancestors.

The Utes have a legend: *The land is the body, the people are the spirit. When the land and the people are cut apart, this is death.*

George A. Jackson

II

PAYDIRT!

The Towns That Boomed
and
The Lucky Ones Who Struck It Rich

* * *

" A cry echoed across the country ---
'PIKES PEAK OR BUST' "

When Lt. Zebulon Pike reached Santa Fe in 1806 he was surprised to find there, as already noted, the Kentucky Mountain Man, James Purcell, who told him about finding gold in South Park. This is the first mention of gold in the Colorado Rockies by an American. Pike was not impressed and scarcely noted the fact in his Journal.

Fifty-three years later, and a decade after gold had been discovered in California, rumors of *gold in them thar hills* filtered back east, and a cry echoed across the country—"Pikes Peak or Bust!" Pikes Peak was the only mountain most easterners had heard of, and they equated Pikes Peak with all the Rockies, and assumed that was where the gold was. Soon long trains of covered wagons were snaking their way across the plains, *Pikes Peak or Bust* bravely painted on the canvas. The St. Louis, Missouri, Republican on March 10, 1859, put the frenzy into perspective: ". . . Pike's Peak figured in a million dreams. . . . There were Pike's Peak hats, Pike's Peak guns, Pike's Peak boots, Pike's Peak goodness-knows-what-all. . . . We presume there will be Pike's Peak goggles to keep the gold dust out of the eyes of the fortune hunters." There was gold, all right, but the seekers didn't find it at Pikes Peak. Not for another 30 years. (Note: Pike and his Peak were always given the possessive apostrophe at this time and for some years later. Now, the mountain is simply *Pikes Peak*.)

Some of the pioneers, in disgust, added the word *BUSTED!* to their banners and turned around and went home. Others, more determined, turned northward along the Front Range to join what was fast becoming a real gold rush along Clear Creek west of Denver.

In May of 1859, Red-Bearded John Gregory had made a rich

John Gregory

strike in Gregory Gulch, and Central City was born in what came to be called the richest square mile on earth. George Jackson found gold on Chicago Creek and the tent camp originally dubbed Jackson's Diggins developed before long into Idaho Springs. Green Russell made his big strike in Russell's Gulch. George Griffith, hearing of all this gold activity, rushed to Gregory Gulch but found all the claims taken; Russell Gulch and Jackson's Diggins were over-populated, too. He drifted further into the hills, stumbled upon rich ore, and the camp that mushroomed was called Georgetown.

Now we've met the men who started it all. Shall we explore the once rip-roaring towns that rapidly grew up around these and later camps, and become acquainted with the fascinating ghosts that haunt them?

CENTRAL CITY

Life was hard in the early mining communities, and entertainments to relax, divert, and amuse came right on the heels of the miners. Jack Langrishe, a genial Irishman with an enormous nose and a powerful voice,

John S. Langrishe

who convulsed his audiences when he played comedy roles, was one of the first troupers in Central City. He had a flair for training miners and dance hall girls to be adequate, if not professional, performers, and his traveling troupes played to enthusiastic audiences in any mining town that could provide a theater, however crude.

One of his early original plays was *Pat Casey's Night Hands*. Now the story goes that while he was digging a grave, Pat struck it rich, and he fell easily into the role of rich man, hiring body-guards and showing off mightily. When it became known that Langrishe had made him the hero of a play, Pat was furious. He almost bought out the theater on opening night, so his men would be on hand to break up the show. Wind of his plans got out and 50 armed vigilantes also attended. However, as the show progressed, Pat and his men became more and more pleased and proud, and it ended with him and his cohorts cheering loudly.

Early in 1861 Jack Langrishe produced "Camille" as the opener for the new Central City Opera House—an ambitious undertaking. In the years

22

that followed, many famous entertainers from the east appeared in Central City. Vaudeville and minstrel shows were eagerly awaited. Lady contortionists were especially popular. After one performance the reviewer just could not find words to describe the twistings and turnings of the star's lithe and lissome body, and ended lamely, "In fact, she was like a boned chicken."

The big fire of 1874 wiped out most of the town and destroyed the theater, but the ardor for culture was not long dampened, and four years later, on March 4, 1878, the present Central City Opera House was opened. The greats of the theater came to the booming mining town in the Colorado Rockies—Sarah Bernhardt, Edwin Booth, Joseph Jefferson, many others. When gold petered out the town became a *ghost* and with it, the Opera House.

One of the contractors for the Opera House had been Peter McFarlane. In 1932 his daughter-in-law, Mrs. Ida Kruse McFarlane, became possessed by an idea—to re-open the Opera House as a summer festival center. Peter McFarlane's heirs gave the building to the University of Denver, and the Central City Opera House Association was formed. For years the Opera House had been boarded up; it was dusty, mouldy, decaying. Water seeping through the leaky roof had ruined or damaged murals and frescoes. Rats claimed the building for their own. To help raise money for cleaning and restoration, memorial chairs were sold. Donors could have the name of a pioneer carved across the back of one of the original hickory chairs. Most of the names one reads in Colorado history are inscribed on these quaint Opera House chairs.

On July 16, 1932, Mrs. McFarlane's dream became a reality—the rejuvenated Central City Opera House opened. It was a nostalgic moment; for the play was, again, *Camille*. Lillian Gish, star of the silent screen, played the heroine. The Central City Summer Festival continues to be one of Colorado's most exciting annual events.

John Evans

Associated with Mrs. McFarlane from the beginning was Miss Anne Evans, daughter of Colorado's second Territorial Governor, Dr. John Evans. Dr. Evans was one of the most remarkable men ever to come to Colorado. When Abraham Lincoln appointed him Governor to succeed William Gilpin, the 48-year-old Evans had already had four successful careers—in medicine, in education, as financier, as railroad builder.

In Attica, Indiana, as a young doctor, he became concerned with the treatment of the blind, the deaf, and the insane, and was instrumental in inducing the State to build an adequate insane asylum and a home and school for deaf-mutes. Before he was 30, his name was known in medical circles as a pioneer in humane and scientific work, and as a contributor to medical journals.

23

Central City photographed approximately 1879, by A. M. Thomas. View west toward hill, looking up Main Street.

Main Street in Central City.

24

While in Attica, he listened to a lecture on Education by Bishop Matthew Simpson of the Methodist Episcopal Church, and this powerful sermon marked a crisis point in his life. He gave up his Quaker beliefs and became a Methodist, and he decided that teaching the mentally competent presented an even greater field for usefulness than humanitarian efforts for the mentally incompetent.

He left Attica and joined the faculty at Rush Medical College in Chicago. Here, in addition to becoming one of the organizers of the American Medical Society, he invented a number of surgical instruments still in use today. Due to his research on cholera, which at one time reached epidemic proportions in parts of the United States, he was largely responsible for passage of the vital National Quarantine Law of 1866.

In Chicago, Dr. Evans master-minded the founding of Northwestern University under the government of the Methodist Episcopal Church, and the site chosen for the school was namel Evanston. The University was to be inter-denominational, open to all qualified students, yet totally subject to Christian government and influence, for, said Dr. Evans, "There is no other cause to which you can more profitably lend your influence, your labor, and your means, than that of Christian education. . . . When we found an institution to mold minds and characters for good . . . we have done the highest and noblest service to our country and our race. . . ."

His Evans Block along the Chicago lakefront was the beginning of that city's massive and beautiful lakefront development. He promoted the Fort Wayne and Chicago Railroad, and his little depot grew into the gigantic Chicago Union Depot, and his rails became one nucleus of the Pennsylvania System.

Dr. Evans now entered politics, and helped organize the Republican Party which nominated Abraham Lincoln. One of Lincoln's first acts as President was to offer the Governorship of Washington Territory to Evans, but he declined—the Pacific coast was too far from his great business and educational interests in Chicago. Then Lincoln offered him the Governorship of Colorado Territory. Evans made the wearying and dangerous 13-day journey from Chicago to Denver in May, 1862. He liked everything he saw—the plains, the mountains, the excitement of the gold rush, the challenge of the frontier. At age 48, at the pinnacle of achievement in several fields, Dr. John Evans became a Colorado pioneer.

The pattern of his life in Chicago was repeated in Denver. He organized the Rocky Mountain Conference of the Methodist Episcopal Church and on the second day resolutions were adopted that led to the founding of Denver University. He helped promote three successful railroads—the Denver Pacific to connect Denver with the Union Pacific at Cheyenne; the Denver, Texas & Gulf; the Denver, South Park & Pacific. Railroad builder; city builder; park system planner and promoter; educator; civic leader—Dr. Evans's multitudinous talents and abilities were all dedicated to the development of his home city, Denver, Colorado.

On his 81st birthday the people of Colorado honored John Evans by naming the third great sentinel of the Front Range, higher than either Longs Peak or Pikes Peak, for him: Mt. Evans.

Dr. Evans' daughter Anne, who did so much to revive Central City, was a worthy heir of this versatile and illustrious man.

* * * * *

By 1872, the citizens of Central City felt it was high time they had a fine hotel. Henry M. Teller, attorney and leading citizen, offered to erect a $20,000 building if the community would furnish the site. By the time Teller House was completed the cost had risen to $87,000. The largest and finest hotel in Colorado (some proud boosters claimed these superlatives should have read "in the entire west") held a gala opening in June, 1872. Its fame and that of Central City would spread far and wide the next year when President Ulysses S. Grant arrived for a visit. The city fathers sent to Caribou, a rich silver camp not far away, for $13,000 worth of silver bricks to pave the sidewalk in front of Teller House for him to walk on. It would have been no special honor to walk on gold bricks in Central City.

Henry M. Teller

The fire of 1874 stopped just short of the strong brick walls of Teller House. Wet blankets hung in the windows helped save the hotel from serious damage.

Henry Teller grew up as a farm lad in upper New York State in the 1840s and '50s with a burning desire for education. At 15 he began teaching in a rural school and reading law. The self-taught lawyer was offered a position with the law firm in Morrison, Illinois, population 455, when he was 28, at just about the time news of gold in the Colorado Rockies was exciting people. The newspaper reported that Morrison was drained of its population as people joined the Pikes Peak or Bust wagon trains rumbling through the town. Teller caught the fever, too, and in 1861 he headed for Central City.

Teller, the prudent and discreet eastern lawyer, was in for many surprises in the Peoples' Courts set up by the miners and presided over by a shirt sleeved, untaught "judge." In one case, the "jury" voted for immediate—and final—justice-by-lynching of a Mexican who had been caught robbing a sluice box of its deposit of gold. When Teller saw he couldn't stop them, he asked that at least the prisoner be given a chance to pray. The thief hooted his disdain of this offer, so Teller himself offered up a respectable petition—and gained fame as a lawyer who tried to get a thief who wasn't good enough for the *Kingdom of Gilpin* into the *Kingdom of Heaven*.

Teller's business activities broadened, and he became the Agent for many easterners who had been persuaded to invest in Colorado's mines, as well as an expert on mining law. Few important civil cases came up in Colorado Territory in which Teller did not have a part. He was instrumental in bringing the narrow-gauge Colorado Central to Black Hawk, and then up the steep grade to Central City.

When Colorado became *The Centennial State* in 1876, Teller and Jerome B. Chaffee, who had been on opposite sides of many questions, were elected by the State Legislature as the first two United States Senators. Then they found that the terms to which they had been elected ran, in one case, only three months, in the other three years. They drew lots, and Teller drew the short term. This situation forced the Legislature to choose a Senator for the six-year term which would follow in three months. They re-elected Teller to the long term, so he won over Chaffee after all. This was the beginning of a 30-year period in Washington for Henry Teller, as Senator, and for three years (1882-1885) as Secretary of the Interior in President Chester A. Arthur's Cabinet.

Colorado, which became the 38th state in 1876, was the youngest state for 13 years; not until 1889 were any new states admitted to the Union. Colorado was surrounded by Territories, each of which had a non-voting delegate in the House of Representatives, but no voice whatever in the Senate. Senator Teller, who had lived through Colorado's territorial period, and who understood territorial problems, felt a special responsibility to these neighboring areas and spoke and acted for them in Washington, becoming *the defender of the West.*

Teller, nationally known as an advocate of free coinage, was seriously considered for nomination for President in 1896 by the Democrats, although he was a "Silver Republican"; and if the Democrats didn't nominate him, a coalition of Silver Republicans and Populists would. Teller, honest man that he was, didn't aid his campaign manager at all, for he kept saying publicly that he thought his nomination was injudicious. The outcome, of course, was that the silver-tongued orator William Jennings Bryan got the nomination and lost to William McKinley.

When Senator Teller, this "ablest representative of the West," was asked if he had written his autobiography, he said, "No . . . my record is my life—I must stand or fall by that."

Henry Teller died in 1914. His family continued to operate Teller House in Central City as a fine hostelry until 1935, when it was purchased by the Central City Opera House Association and made into a museum. Its decor and furnishings are redolent of the opulence of life in Central City when it was the sparkling jewel of *the richest square mile on earth.*

BLACK HAWK

The early prospectors went up the streams feverishly panning for gold, dipping up a pan of water and silt, watching breathlessly to see if any heavier gold sank to the bottom. This gold in the streams had come from a mother lode in the hills, and as the gold in the streams played out, the prospectors took picks and hacked away at the rocks seeking these gold veins. But these men were not miners, nor were their tools adequate for hard-rock mining. They devised primitive stamp mills to crush the ore and release the gold, but these were so inefficient that much good ore was left in the dumps. As mining in the hills developed, much of the complex

27

Blackhawk, where Gregory Gulch and Clear Creek come together.

Nathaniel Hill, standing in the doorway, proudly views the silver bullion just produced by his Boston & Colorado Gold and Silver Smelting Co., Blackhawk, 1873. Dr. Richard Pierce, far left, was superintendent.

ore was sent across the Atlantic, to Swansea, Wales, for the gold, silver, and other valuable minerals to be separated.

In 1864 Nathaniel P. Hill, a chemistry professor, visited Gregory Gulch, saw the frustrating and expensive problems the miners were having, and set out to do something about it. Like Henry Teller, Nathaniel Hill had been a farm boy in New York state who was determined to acquire an education. Very early he showed great skill in chemistry, and by the time he was 27, in 1859, he was a full Professor of Chemistry at his Alma Mater, Brown University.

After his visit to Colorado he began to study the problems of ore reduction. He made two trips to Europe, especially to Swansea, where he watched critically every step in processing a special shipment of Colorado ores. When Hill was sure he had a workable process developed, he persuaded eastern capitalists to finance a company to build a smelter at Black Hawk, and the Boston-Colorado Smelter Works began operation in 1868. The ore treatment plant revolutionized the mining industry in Colorado. Soon smelters modeled after Hill's were operating full blast throughout the state.

From now on, Hill was a resident of Colorado. When Jerome B. Chaffee announced that because of ill health he would not be a candidate for reelection as Senator at the end of his three-year term (in 1879), Hill was nominated by the Republicans and elected by the State Legislature. Five years later, Hill was up for reelection; but the Legislature chose to return Henry Teller, who was just ending his term as Secretary of the Interior, back to the Senate, replacing Hill. Hill's anger knew no bounds. Some time before, he had established a newspaper, the Denver Republican; and from now on he never missed an opportunity to use this medium to put Teller in a bad light.

However, Teller was to return good for evil. Some far-sighted individuals were becoming alarmed at the exploitation of America's forests and demanded that they be conserved for the future. Carl Schurz, then Secretary of the Interior, decided to prosecute westerners who removed timber from public lands. There was hardly a miner, settler, railroad, church, or even private citizen who was not technically a violator of the law. One suit that was filed was for $100,000 against Nathaniel P. Hill's Smelter at Black Hawk. Hill forgot his animosity and appealed to Teller, *the Defender of the West.* Teller pointed out to Schurz that there was no way for people of the west to get wood except to go upon the public lands for it, and succeeded in securing passage of the *Timber Cutting Act* making it legal for anyone except a railroad corporation to take timber for any purposes except export, and the suit against Hill was dropped.

If the suit had gone through the courts and the chemist-professor-smelter owner-newspaperman-Senator had lost, the $100,000 would hardly have been missed out of the large fortune Nathaniel P. Hill had already accumulated in Colorado.

GEORGETOWN

Almost from the beginning Georgetown was a discriminating and refined city. The man who did most to set this aristocratic tone was the mysterious Frenchman, Louis Dupuy, and his splendid Hotel de Paris. Dupuy, who had come to Georgetown as a miner, was injured in an accident while saving another miner's life. The citizens collected a purse for him, and with the money he purchased a bakery which, by 1875, he had developed into the elegant Hotel de Paris. The Hotel became the center of Georgetown social life and was famous throughout the nation.

Louis Dupuy

Though the mystery about Dupuy was never fully solved, it was rumored that he had been born to wealth and position in France, but had squandered his inheritance and had drifted through a variety of occupations before reaching Georgetown. Whatever his history, the discriminating taste of a cultured man was everywhere in evidence in his hotel. The decor was lavishly Parisian— gilt mirrors, sculpture, paintings, fine furniture, handsome draperies.

Dupuy held high standards of conduct and good taste, and he didn't hesitate to evict anyone who violated them. He has been described variously as an innkeeper who hated his guests, a philosopher, an aristocrat, a pagan, an atheist, a lover of beauty, and a despiser of women. True, he said he hated women; yet a woman, Madame Sophie Galet, his housekeeper, gradually took over operation of the Hotel and dominated his life. When he died in 1900 he left everything to her; when she died a few months later, she was buried beside him. Carved on the tombstone over the double grave are the words *Deux Bons Amis — Two Good Friends.*

Dupuy not only had his philosophies concerning man, but concerning food as well. Once when a guest said rapturously that he would like slave girls and music with dessert, and with his wine would have orange blossoms and roses fall upon the table, M. Dupuy proudly responded that with *his* wines, one smelled the scent of the roses and imagined the slave girls!

* * * * *

Another notable citizen of Georgetown was William A. Hamill. He, too, was an European, born in England in 1836. He came to the U.S. as a young man, fought in the Civil War, then came west as a prospector. Gradually he acquired some of the richest mines in the Georgetown area, including the *Pelican.* Another mine, the *Dives,* tapped the same vein, and this caused plenty of trouble. At one time there were more than 20 suits and counter-suits pending between the two mining companies. The Pelican finally won—but the Dives had the last word. One day a sad procession of miners emerged from the Dives, carrying six coffins and telling of a tragic accident. The coffins seemed unduly heavy. They were—they contained high grade ore. Finally Mr. Hamill acquired also the Dives, and a little later sold both for $5,000,000, making him the richest man in the region.

He spent much of his wealth making his home a luxurious showplace (it is now a museum). He imported Carrara marble for the fireplaces; flocked wallpaper with gold, silver, and camel's hair for the parlor; unusual chandeliers. Off the dining room was a curved glass solarium with an elaborate fountain and flower-stand in the center. The mammoth walnut desk in his office, a beautifully-proportioned building made of native granite at the rear of the garden, was trimmed with gold and silver inlay. Everything spoke of richness in abundance.

Though he never studied law, Hamill became an outstanding authority on mining laws, and was a state political and civic leader.

The silver crash of 1893 broke Hamill, as it did so many others. He died in 1904, a comparatively poor man.

* * * * *

A rare character touching the Georgetown area was "Brick" Pomeroy. He was one of Colorado's colossal characters, and one of the most talked-about men of his day. He spread himself thin on many ambitious enterprises, but his giant project was the Atlantic-Pacific Tunnel. The idea was to bore through Gray's Peak south of Georgetown, thought to be the narrowest point under the Continental Divide. The railroad tunnel,

Mark M. Pomeroy

projected to be 25,000 feet long, would cut some 100 miles off the distance between Denver and Leadville.

Brick traveled across America and to Europe to win financial support for the tunnel. Shares sold at $2.50 each, and they went so fast the company could hardly keep up with printing them. It's estimated Brick raised between two and four million dollars; and work started at both ends of the tunnel.

The financial panic of 1893 brought things to a halt at the tunnel, and Brick Pomeroy's financial structure began to tumble. Stockholders asked to see the company's books, but Brick refused both individuals and a court order. He was indicted for malfeasance in office, but the case never came to trial—too many big people were involved for it ever to become a public scandal.

Before his fertile mind began to dream up far-out schemes, Brick had been a newspaper man and writer, and was popular as a lecturer and after-dinner speaker. His books, *Sense; Nonsense; Gold Dust; Brick Dust;* and others, published in the 70s, expressed his liberal viewpoint and were unmercifully panned by conservatives. However, after his death in 1896, even Nathaniel Hill's ultra-conservative Denver Republican wrote, "It is safe to say that no man ever brought more money into Colorado or scattered it more broadcast over the state."

31

The famous Georgetown Loop, between Georgetown and Silver Plume. This was the Colorado Central, later the Union Pacific, Denver and Gulf, then the Colorado and Southern R.R.

Georgetown's finest turn out to race their firefighting equipment. These races were regular Fourth of July events.

Thirty years later the famed Moffat tunnel was being dug under the Continental Divide west of Denver, and the Mountain States Monitor said, "(This work will) justify the hopes and result in the completion of the plans that Brick Pomeroy and David H. Moffat carried with them to the 'great divide' which they have already crossed. Mankind would make slow progress without men of this type."

* * * * *

"Commodore" Stephen Decatur was one of the most popular men in Georgetown. He was not the Commodore of "my country right or wrong" fame, but a man whose real name was Stephen Decatur Bross. He wasn't the only man to come west to lose his identity.

He was a school teacher in New York, when he suddenly disappeared in the 1840s, leaving a wife and two children behind. There was a repeat performance in Nebraska, where he left another wife and child. By now he had dropped the surname, Bross. He fought in the Mexican War, he fought the Indians, he had many adventures here and there, and finally he came to Colorado. By the time we meet him in Georgetown, the Commodore had inevitably attached itself to his name, and he was a favorite orator called on to preach from the pulpit, perform the last rites at a burial, present medals, even speak on temperance, though he dearly loved his liquor.

In 1876, the country celebrated its Centennial and Colorado, The Centennial State, was taken into the Union as the 38th state; Decatur was appointed to represent Colorado at the Centennial Exposition in Philadelphia. The state appropriation petered out, but Decatur kept the Colorado exhibit open at his own expense, using up most of his fortune. He died, penniless, at Rosita in the Wet Mountain Valley, where the kindly citizens fed and looked after him.

Grace Greenwood, noted author and lecturer, met "Commodore" Stephen Decatur in Colorado in 1873, and it is said he told her the true story of his life. If so, she never revealed it, saying she was too busy—and too honorable—to tell. But she made it clear that she thought he was one of the most interesting men she'd ever met.

SILVER PLUME

In the book she wrote describing her travels in Colorado, Miss Greenwood gave the rules of the Silver Plume Hotel: "No lights allowed in the rooms after the candles have burned out"; and, "If you wish water, the creek is 70 yards south and the pail is in the kitchen."

If conditions downtown in Silver Plume were rough, they must have been much worse up on the mountain-side where Clifford Griffin had his cabin. Griffin, an Englishman, came to Silver Plume in the '60s, climbed the mountain back of the town, and discovered the 7:30, one of the richest. He built his cabin close by the mine. Little was known of the lonely man. It was whispered that he had murdered his fiancee the evening before their scheduled wedding, and had fled to the far-off mountains of Colorado to escape the law. No one really knew, so everyone surmised.

However it happened, for years he lived on the mountain-side, digging in his mine during the day, playing his violin in the evening. At dusk the soft strains of his music wafted down to the villagers below. One evening in 1887 as he ended his concert, they heard a shot. They rushed up the mountain and found the miner-musician, a bullet through his heart, lying in a newly-dug grave. These past few weeks he had not been digging for ore; he had been preparing his final resting place—a place where he might, at last, find the peace and solace that even the mountains had not brought him.

* * * * *

A prominent feature of Clear Creek Canon was W. A. H. Loveland's Colorado Central Railroad, many traces of which can still be seen. Built to serve the mining camps of Black Hawk, Central City, Idaho Springs, Georgetown and Silver Plume, the road carried much ore and machinery. It also became famous as a tourist attraction. On this line connecting Georgetown and Silver Plume was the famous Georgetown Loop, the nearest thing to a roller coaster that Colorado had for years, with its 14 curves, some of them dizzily spiralling over similar curves below, and its high trestles looking like flimsy spider webs. The towns are 1¾ miles apart though the railroad took 4½ miles to gain the 623 feet difference in altitude between them. The high bridge was 300 feet long and rose 90 feet above the stream. The Loop ranked with Niagara Falls and Yellowstone as a magnet for vacationers. Today the Loop is being rebuilt by the Colorado Historical Society. Trains will run over it again.

Placering near Breckenridge. This mining technique preceeded the dredges—both account for the scars on hills and streams around Breckenridge, Central City and other mining camps.

Georgetown, circa 1895 when the population was listed at 2,000 people.

Peter Haldi, Blacksmith, Altona, Boulder Canyon. Photo was taken near the turn of the century.

III.

RICH ORE FURTHER WEST

LEADVILLE

" Here were men to match these mountains "

he saga of the Tabors of Leadville might well be the Great American Tragedy. Here is the very essence of drama and tragedy: The love, the heartaches, the passion, the sudden rise to riches and then, just as suddenly, financial catastrophe; the final irony. Consider—

The Cast of Characters:

Horace Austin Warner Tabor, middle-aged storekeeper who suddenly strikes it rich and feels the urge to splurge.

Augusta, his frugal New England wife, who is satisfied with things as they are in her small home in Leadville.

Baby Doe, beautiful young divorcee with whom Tabor falls in love at sight and marries.

Rosemary Silver Dollar Echo and Elizabeth Pearl, their daughters, one of whom, Silver Dollar, falls to the lowest depths and dies in a Chicago gutter; the other, who repudiates both her name and family.

H.A.W. Tabor

Synopsis:

Scene I: Horace Tabor was a stonecutter in Vermont, and married Augusta, the daughter of his boss. They heard the call of the open spaces and homesteaded in Kansas; then the call of gold in 1859 lured them to the Rockies. They tried Gregory Gulch, and finding nothing, moved on, oxen pulling their wagon and Horace and Augusta pushing it over the steep grades. Baby Maxcy was teething and sick much of the time. Theirs was the first wagon through to Idaho Springs and Augusta the first woman. Still no gold. In disgust, Horace gave up prospecting and the little family followed the rushes from place to place, he opening up stores, Augusta turning their rough shacks into boarding houses in half a dozen new mining camps.

Augusta L. Tabor

By 1878, Tabor had become a prosperous storekeeper and mayor of Leadville. He grubstaked two miners, giving them $64 in provisions, for a third interest in any strikes. They discovered the *Little Pittsburg*, and he bought them out. In six months, the mine netted Tabor half a million. This was the magic key to untold riches. The *Chrysolite*, the *Matchless*, many other rich mines, poured wealth on the Tabors. He felt the urge to splurge. He built the elegant Tabor Opera House where, on the gas-lighted stage, the dramas of passion, the comedies of sophistication, and the music of operas, were performed to enthralled audiences. He arrayed the Highland Guards, the Light Cavalry (of which he was general), and the fire brigade in fancy uniforms.

Augusta, who had stuck by him and given him encouragement and love during the hard, lean years, was left out of his gay life; and she began to feel lonely and unwanted. Her pride in his becoming Lieutenant Governor turned to hurt when he went about his political, as well as his business, life with scarcely a glance in her direction. He bought a fine mansion in Denver in which Augusta felt lost; he built the Tabor Block and an ornate Opera House in Denver without even consulting her. The income of $100,000 a month did not bring happiness to Augusta.

Scene II: In Oshkosh, Wisconsin, young Harvey Doe, son of the mayor, married beauteous 17-year-old Elizabeth McCourt, and they went to Central City, hoping to strike it rich. But it was not to be: Harvey became a miner, not a millionaire. So pretty was young Elizabeth that the miners called her *Baby* Doe, and thought Harvey the luckiest miner alive. But the Doe household was not a happy one, and the two separated.

Everyone who came to Central City spread the legend of Tabor of Leadville. Baby Doe wanted to see this great man for herself, and she went to The Cloud City.

Baby Doe

She saw a tall, well-dressed man with piercing black eyes and flaring mustachios, a spring in his step despite his 50 years. And he saw her.

Scene III: He demanded a divorce from Augusta and she gave it, sadly, reluctantly. Tabor was appointed Senator for 30 days to fill out the unexpired term of Henry M. Teller. During this time in Washington, he married Baby Doe in one of the most flamboyant weddings of all time. The men who were invited, including President Chester Arthur, came; but their scandalized wives refused to attend.

The following ten years overflowed with riches and happiness, though the Tabors were scorned by Denver society. Two daughters were born to them.

Scene IV: The silver collapse of 1893 brought financial disaster to the Tabors. In the years that followed, Tabor could hardly support his family, though he was finally made Postmaster of Denver. He became ill, and, knowing death was imminent, he gave a final charge to Baby Doe: "Hang on to the Matchless." Then he died, age 69.

Scene V: Baby Doe, following his charge literally, lived out 35 bitter years as a recluse in the cabin beside the shaft of the *Matchless* in Leadville. In March, 1935, people suddenly realized they had not seen the ghost-like Mrs. Tabor in some time. They went to the cabin and found her frozen body, dead several days.

Epilogue: The final irony—Augusta, the rejected wife, died a wealthy and respected, though ever lonely, woman.

[The Tabor story was made into an opera, *The Ballad of Baby Doe,* by Douglas Moore, with libretto by John Latouche, and the world premiere was presented at the Central City Opera House on July 7, 1956. It was acclaimed as "an event to live in musical history."]

Baby Doe taken in front of the Matchless Mine, 1933, still guarding her heritage.

38

*   *   *   *   *

If the Tabor story is the *Great American Tragedy,* then Mollie Brown's is the comic relief.

Mollie Brown

Mollie Tobin came to Leadville at the beginning of the boom with her rough, tough, Irish father and brothers. She married one of the miners, Jimmy J. Brown, who soon struck it rich in the *Little Jonny* mine. Dreams of grandeur began to float through Mollie's agile brain, and her eyes took on a far-away look. She persuaded Jimmy to move to Denver, where they purchased a fine mansion, the House of the Lions, for the lions couchant that guarded the steps. Mollie was determined to crash the Sacred 36 of Denver society. She put on (she thought) the trappings of a lady—but the elite of Denver only laughed at her pretensions, and otherwise ignored her. Her invitations went unanswered; her soirees attended only by the curious. Mollie shook her fist, swore that Denver society would accept her some day, left Jimmy, and went to New York, determined to acquire the refinement obviously necessary for acceptance by society.

Soon, with her good looks, her beautiful clothes, her rapidly-acquired culture—and her money—she became a popular member of New York and Newport society. She went to Europe, traveled with the international set, hobnobbed with royalty, and, like several hundred other socialites, she booked passage back to New York on the maiden voyage of the splendid new ship, the Titanic. About midnight on April 14, 1912, the Titanic hit an iceberg. Women and children were rushed into the inadequately few lifeboats; 1500 men went down with the ship. Mollie took charge of her lifeboat and brought the terrified, freezing passengers through the night and to rescue the next day.

On reaching New York, Mollie, now not only a celebrity but a heroine as well, was asked by the reporters, "Mrs. Brown, how did it happen *you* didn't sink?" "Hell," answered Mollie, "I'm unsinkable." And as *The Unsinkable Mollie Brown* she has gone down in history.

*   *   *   *   *

Another of the legendary Carbonate Kings of Leadville was James Viola Dexter, a small man with a big heart. He was a lover of sports, both outdoor and indoor, and built five hunting lodges, fixing one up as the most exclusive private poker club in Colorado. This particular cabin, looking like any log cabin outside, now sits on the lawn of Healy House Museum at Leadville. The game room, though small, has elaborately decorated walls of leather-like Lincrusta stamped from hand-cut wood blocks, a

James V. Dexter

splendid chandelier, hand-painted window shades, and elegant furnishings.

Dexter became a world traveler, an art and curio collector, and filled seven rooms of his Union Bank Building in Denver with rare bric-a-brac. His coin collection alone was worth over $100,000. When he died in 1899, and his will was read, the executors were directed to a certain key. Hidden in a trunk which this key opened were found selected gifts from his fabulous collections, each tagged with the name of one of his many friends, to be delivered on the Christmas after his death, whenever it might occur. What great fun he must have had choosing just the right gift to surprise and please a particular person after he, himself, was but a memory.

* * * * *

Many a famous fortune had its beginnings in Leadville—the Guggenheims of Philadelphia; Samuel Newhouse, whose lucky strike enabled him to hobnob with the Prince of Wales and to become one of the largest copper operators in the world; Alva Adams, three times elected governor of Colorado; Charles Boettcher, one of Colorado's wealthiest financiers; John F. Campion, who later developed the beet sugar industry in Colorado. And then there was John Morrissey, illiterate and ignorant, but rich. When promoters of Twin Lakes as a summer resort talked of bringing in Venetian-type gondolas, they asked Morrissey how many he thought they should purchase. "Just get a couple and let 'em breed," he advised. Morrissey was no mathematician. One day he yelled down his mine, "How many of yez are down there?" The answer echoed up, "Three." "Well," ordered Morrissey, "Half of yez come up and have a drink."

* * * * *

It seemed that all was over in Leadville after 1893. In that year President Cleveland repealed the Sherman Silver Purchase Act, which meant that the federal government would no longer buy silver as a backing for its currency. About the same time India ceased buying silver for its currency, thereby cutting off most of the foreign market. The Carbonate Kings lost their fortunes almost overnight.

But Leadville survived. The hills were still full of minerals waiting to be mined. There was, for instance, molybdenum. In 1879, Charles Senter, prospecting on Bartlett Mountain at the top of Fremont Pass, staked out a claim to an outcrop of bluish-gray ore that looked like lead. (Leadville and the Carbonate Kings had received their names because the silver that made them rich had been found in carbonate of lead.) He took samples of the ore to the assayers, who said it was a poor grade of graphite and virtually worthless. In 1890, however, scientists identified it as a little-

40

Chestnut Street, Leadville.

Strikes in Colorado mines were frequent and bloody and won by the mine owners. Usually the State Militia was brought in to settle the dispute, as in this case, Leadville, 1896.

known mineral named *molybdenum* from a Greek word meaning lead-like. No one knew of any particular use for it, so the deposits lay idle.

The first attempt to commercially exploit this vast deposit of molybdenite was made by Otis A. King. He negotiated an option to purchase with Senter as early as 1913; but found no market for the metal, and no way to extract it.

Later, after forming the Pingrey Mines and Ore Reduction Co., in Leadville, King resumed negotiations with Senter and obtained a new series of options on Senter's claims on Bartlett Mountain.

George Backus, mill superintendent for King and the Pingrey company, found a way to successfully recover the extremely low-grade ore—through the new technique of selective flotation. In the fall of 1915, King shipped the first commercial run of molybdenum concentrate, 5,824 pounds, thought to be an 18 months supply for the world. This was reported in the U.S. Government publication, *Mineral Resources*.

It was at this time that Max Schott arrived on the scene. He had come to the U.S. from Germany, in 1893, when he was 17. His first job was as office boy in German Gesellschaft of New York, a German holding company with extensive western hemisphere mineral interests.

Schott's ability to learn was so evident, that he received rapid advancement. In 1907, he was sent to Colorado, and ended up as manager of Gesellschaft's Ohio & Colorado Smelter at Salida.

In August, 1914, Germany opened World War I. Soon Krupp gun designers discovered that the steel in their big guns failed after only a few shots. But Krupp metallurgists found that the addition of small amounts of molybdenum improved the steel cannons so they could take the pounding required. At last, there was now a market for molybdenum. Krupp sent out its message for the metal and a recipient of this order was German Gesellschaft of New York. The story in *Mineral Resources*, reporting Kings shipment of molybdenum ore, had not gone unnoticed and in early 1916, Gesellschaft of New York gave its man in Colorado an order to get Bartlett Mountain. Schott employed gun-toting claim jumpers and the U.S. courts to mount one of Colorado's biggest battles for control of a mining property.

In January 1918, to assuage the high running anti-German sentiment, German Gesellschaft of New York changed its name to American Metals Company. Again, this German company met with a war imposed problem—the Alien Properties Act, passed after the U.S. entered World War I. On Feb. 3, 1918, shares of American Metals held by enemy stock holders were siezed by the alien property custodian, who also named five directors of the company. This expropriation amounted to 40% of the stock of American Metals Company, sufficient to control the company. However, Max Schott remained head of the Colorado operations.

In this same month of February, American Metals' new Colorado subsidiary, Climax Molybdenum Company, shipped its first concentrates. Later that year Schott settled out of court with Otis King and American Metals Co., through Climax Molybdenum Co., owned Bartlett Mountain.

Almost coincident with the end of the war, demand for molybdenum dropped to zero. Finally, the Climax mill was shut down, and remained closed until 1924, when it was reopened by limited production, not to go into full operation until World War II. Schott, however, never lived to see the final success of the company.

Because of its high melting point (4750° F.), moly is used in hardening and toughening steels and cast iron and in making many of today's vital materials. Nearly 300,000,000 tons of ore have been drawn from Bartlett Mountain, leaving a gigantic *glory hole*. Only a fraction of usable mineral is recovered from each ton of ore, and the waste material is disposed of in immense tailing ponds that fill the valleys below Climax.

Max Schott's determination and persistence paid off handsomely. Today the Climax Molybdenum Company dominates things around Leadville. The Company comes by its name because in the early days the top of Fremont pass marked the climax of the long uphill pull made by the puffing little steam trains on their way from Denver to Leadville.

Moly, in the form of an attractive young maiden, points the way, on signs, to Leadville from all directions.

EAST FROM LEADVILLE

East from Leadville are a number of mining towns, some dead, some alive. Back in '59, miners panned gold in Michigan Creek in South Park and decided to tarry there long enough to get all the gold out of the

One of the culprits responsible for the rock piles around Breckenridge. This is the Reliance dredge, commissioned by Ben Stanley Revett in 1905, shown operating in French Gulch.

stream. In fact, they called their camp *Tarryall*. The news leaked out, and other fortune hunters came rushing in. The original Tarryallers were so inhospitable that the newcomers opined the name ought to be *Graball,* and went on a few miles to establish their own camp—which they named *Fairplay.*

Across the stream from Tarryall was Hamilton, whose few citizens would like to have had a footbridge connecting the two camps. But the proud Tarryallers thought anyone foolish enough to want to go to Hamilton *should* get his feet wet, and refused to allow the bridge to be built.

On a little stream, the beginning of the South Platte River, was Buckskin Joe, picturesquely named for the leather clothing Joe Higgenbottom wore. A mountain was named for one citizen of Buckskin Joe—Silverheels. Silverheels was a pretty dance hall girl, and when one of the miners made her a pair of slippers with silver heels, her own identity was lost, and she was known only—and affectionately—as Silverheels.

A smallpox epidemic hit Buckskin Joe, and Silverheels was a good angel to the miners and their families, nursing the stricken and comforting the dying . She caught the disease herself, and disappeared.

In later years a heavily-veiled woman returned to Buckskin Joe and walked, ghost-like, through the town and the cemetery. It was Silverheels, her beauty marred by the dread disease, her pocked face hidden by the black veil. Legend or truth? Who knows? Whether the story is part of Colorado's mythical or factual history doesn't really matter; Silverheels Mountain is there to remind us all of the innate goodness in nearly everyone.

At the north end of Hoosier Pass is Breckenridge on the Blue River. Paralleling the town to the west, and extending for miles beyond, is an

Ben S. Revett

extraordinary sight: On both sides of the stream are walls of rocks 20 or more feet high—a stark background for the gay-nineties style buildings that line the main street. These continuous piles of rocks were made by the giant dredges brought into the area about the turn of the century. They cut wide swaths in the streams, dredging to bedrock, floating on the ponds they themselves created as they inched forward, the machinery crushing the rock, washing it down a sluice from which the heavier gold dropped into collection boxes, ejecting the waste rock out the back end. Dredging was the ultimate extension of panning for gold— 40 men working a giant machine in the mountain streams, as against one man with one pan watching eagerly for pay dirt. During World War II, most of these dredges, which cost close to a million dollars each, were sold for scrap metal.

Dredging for gold was introduced by Ben S. Revett, who lived near

Tiger-on-the-Swan, the Swan being a tributary of the Blue. Ben weighed close to 300 pounds, and the doors of his home, *Swan's Nest*, were enlarged accordingly. The general sentiment among laborers who sometimes moonlighted as gravediggers was the hope that when genial Ben met his death it would be near the graveyard!

In the early days it was felt by many that there must be a water-way connection between the Rockies and the Pacific, and in 1869 Sam Adams thought he had a feasible route figured out. He persuaded the citizens of Breckenridge to finance a navy, and the ladies embroidered a fancy banner for the flagship: "Western Colorado to California—Greetings."

By mid-summer all was ready, and Cap'n Sam and his fleet (four flatboats and ten seamen) had a gay send-off down the Blue River. Before the fleet got anywhere near the Colorado River, the boats had broken up, the seamen had mutinied, and Captain Sam wandered back, a disillusioned man.

Not only did Breckenridge claim the distinction of having the only navy ever floated in Colorado; it has an even more bizarre claim to fame: During all its mining boom-and-bust days, it was not even a part of the United States, much less of Colorado. It seems that when the United States was purchasing land from the Indians, a large surrounding area was inadvertently left out and still, theoretically, at least, belonged to the Indians. When this surprising discovery was made in 1936, Governor Ed Johnson ceremoniously raised the flags of the state and the nation over Breckenridge and officially welcomed this "foreign territory" into the union. Breckenridge still retains the right, however, to be an "independent kingdom" for three days each year.

ASPEN

Judge Davis H. Waite

One of Aspen's best known citizens became nationally famous for making a most unfortunate statement. He was Judge Davis H. Waite, later to be elected governor of Colorado on the Populist ticket in 1892. He was instrumental in founding the Party, its primary platform being a return to Bimetallism, the use of both gold and silver as a backing for currency. A year after his election (1893), silver lost, when President Cleveland repealed the Sherman Silver Purchase Act.

The same year labor troubles broke out between the Western Federation of Miners and the mine owners in a number of places, most violently in Cripple Creek. The governor, paraphrasing the 20th verse of the 14th Chapter of Revelation, which reads, "and the winepress was trodden without the city, and blood came out of the winepress even unto the horse bridles," said, "It were better that blood should flow to the horses'

45

bridles than that our national liberties should be destroyed." Newspapers ignored the source, the intent, and the Biblical wording, and headlined, "Governor says, 'Let blood flow to the horses' bridles!' " Waite was razzed, ridiculed, and vilified, depending on the temper and the politics of the assailant. The New York Tribune took the razzing approach, asking him, in an editorial, if he knew that European potentates were so disturbed by his speech that they kept the Atlantic cable so hot with their inquiries about him that parboiled whales were turning belly-up all the way across.

Despite the fact that he handled the strike fairly and brought about a relatively non-violent settlement favoring the union miners, Governor Davis H. Waite will be forever remembered as *Bloody Bridles Waite.*

*   *   *   *   *

B. Clark Wheeler, who put Aspen on the map—literally—was a man of unquenchable optimism and enthusiasm. When rumors filtered into

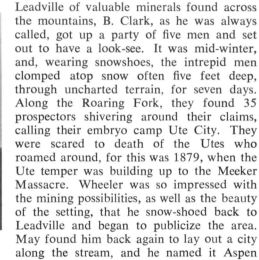

B. Clark Wheeler

Leadville of valuable minerals found across the mountains, B. Clark, as he was always called, got up a party of five men and set out to have a look-see. It was mid-winter, and, wearing snowshoes, the intrepid men clomped atop snow often five feet deep, through uncharted terrain, for seven days. Along the Roaring Fork, they found 35 prospectors shivering around their claims, calling their embryo camp Ute City. They were scared to death of the Utes who roamed around, for this was 1879, when the Ute temper was building up to the Meeker Massacre. Wheeler was so impressed with the mining possibilities, as well as the beauty of the setting, that he snow-shoed back to Leadville and began to publicize the area. May found him back again to lay out a city along the stream, and he named it Aspen for the forests thereabouts.

The only bridge across the Roaring Fork was a log laid from bank to bank. B. Clark lost no time in erecting a railing along it and charging 25¢ per person to cross.

His great contribution to Aspen was in calling attention of capitalists to the undeveloped resources of this Colorado wonderland. He did this mainly by giving lectures titled *Aspen Over The Range,* in which he described eloquently the richness of the newly-discovered mining field. He bought up mining claims for himself and acted as agent for people who responded to his salesmanship, buying other claims for them.

B. Clark had been a teacher, lawyer, geologist, and mountaineer before becoming the founder of Aspen. His was a lusty personality, and he expressed himself forcefully in the Aspen Times, which he established soon after coming to the valley between Aspen and Smuggler mountains.

Looking northwest, down Mill Street in Aspen, from Aspen Mountain, now the ski area. The time is 1890.

Aspen's Hotel Jerome, opened in November, 1889. Built by Jerome B. Wheeler, who simultaneously built the still-standing Wheeler Grand Opera House.

Periodically he enlarged the Times. On one such occasion, in 1888, the Denver World, in a congratulatory editorial, good-naturedly told it like it was about B. Clark Wheeler. "A saint," opined the World, "couldn't live within a mile of B. Clark Wheeler without getting in a row with him, but we will not deny the devil his due, and from the bottom of our heart we acknowledge the man a hero, with temper cut on the bias, but a hero just the same."

And hero he was to Aspen and its residents. Especially to the daughter of Judge Davis H. Waite, who became his bride in 1883.

* * * * *

Another man named Wheeler, but no relative, played an equally important role in Aspen's colorful life. Jerome B. Wheeler, president of Macy & Company of New York, caught the Aspen fever after a visit in

1883. He brought a fortune with him, and added other millions to it as he bought up productive mines. Not all easterners were willing to invest in mining, for it could happen that their coined dollars would disappear in the high costs of searching for the uncoined silver bouillon. But Mr. Wheeler fell in love with the Colorado mountains, and it was fortunate for Aspen that he chose to spend his money there. He spent generously and his ideas were a boon to the rapidly-growing community.

He built a smelter at the foot of the mountains and an electric tramway to bring the ores down to it. (Aspen was the first city in Colorado to have electric lights.) He provided Aspen with the splendid Wheeler Opera House and the opulent Jerome Hotel, each at a cost of close to a million dollars.

Jerome B. Wheeler

The social elite, dressed as stylishly as though they were in the center of the eastern fashion world instead of 2000 miles away in the heart of the mountains of Colorado, left their handsome residences to dine at the Jerome, where the cuisine was excellent and the menu choices wide. Seafood delicacies shipped in from both coasts were a specialty; the cellar was well stocked with the finest imported wines. Living was truly lavish in Aspen.

Jerome Wheeler invested heavily in James J. Hagerman's Colorado Midland Railroad. An exciting race by the railroads kept everyone keyed up in late 1887. The Denver & Rio Grande was rushing to bring its narrow gauge line the 42 miles up the Roaring Fork from Glenwood Springs to Aspen; the Colorado Midland was battling the elements and the granite to open the Hagerman Tunnel and bring its broad gauge rails in from Leadville. The Baby Railroad made it first, puffing into Aspen on November 1, 1887, and Aspen was deliriously happy. It greeted the special train carrying President David Moffat of the D&RG, Governor

Alva Adams, Senator Henry Teller, and other dignitaries with bursts of rockets and Roman candles fired from mine openings that showered the mountains with brilliant cascading light, and put on a great celebration in the Chinese-lantern illuminated streets.

The inevitable anonymous poet memorialized the occasion:

"Then here's to our Aspen, her youth and her age,
We welcome the railroad, say farewell to the stage;
And whatever our lot and wherever we be,
Here's God bless forever the D&RG."

Dairy cows were so frightened by the shriek of the steam whistle and all the commotion that they stopped giving milk, and Aspen residents were on short rations for several days.

James J. Hagerman

The Midland made it two months later, the first standard gauge railroad to cross the Continental Divide.

James J. Hagerman, who built the Colorado Midland, was another Aspen silver millionaire. Like Jerome Wheeler, he had brought a fortune with him to Colorado, made in his Menominee Mining Company in northern Michigan. (Over and over it happened that the future builders of Colorado, in their first jobs as boys, found their proper niche. So it was with Hagerman, whose start was with a company making rails for roadbeds.)

Unlike Wheeler, however, Hagerman came to Colorado a sick man, a victim of tuberculosis. The warm sunshine and pure air brought about a cure, and he went on to make new fortunes in Leadville and Aspen.

There was no way to get the ores out of Aspen except by heavy, cumbersome, mule-drawn wagons that rumbled slowly over trails crossing precarious mountain passes, at a cost of $50 to $100 a ton. Lower grade ores weren't touched because of the high cost of shipping them out. J.J. decided to build a railroad to do the job—for around $15 a ton. The Colorado Midland was soon on the drawing boards, and in short order was on the rails heading from Colorado Springs to Leadville, and from Leadville to Aspen, through the Hagerman Tunnel. The tunnel was 2,164 feet long, at an altitude of 11,528 feet, the highest altitude obtained by a standard gauge road in the U.S. The rails went straight through the tunnel, but the approaches thrilled tourists with breathtaking curves and spidery trestles and steep grades requiring three or four engines to pull the trains.

Jerome Wheeler lost everything in the financial crash of 1893. By 1901 he was forced into bankruptcy, listing half a million in assets and a million and a half in debts. Of all the things he lost, the Wheeler Opera

49

Colorado Midland Rail Road, built by James J. Hagerman. This is the famous loop near Hagerman's Tunnel, where you see a triple loop of ascending railroad.

Saloon in Creede when it was still a tent city.

House brought him the greatest sorrow, for it was his favorite possession. James J. Hagerman went on to make still more millions in Cripple Creek gold, naming his company the Isabella Mining Company because, 'tis said, he formed it in 1892, the 400th anniversary of the discovery of America by Christopher Columbus, "who had been grubstaked by Queen Isabella of Spain."

REDSTONE

On a hillside above the Crystal River some 30 miles west of Aspen is Cleveholm, the 42-room manor-house of a Colorado man whose ideas were far ahead of his time. Along the river banks below the mansion stretched the village of Redstone, one man's dream of what an industrial city could be.

John Cleveland Osgood (the city of Cleveland, Ohio, was named for one of his ancestors) came to Colorado in the early 1880s looking for coal deposits. He organized the Colorado Fuel Company, then bought General William J. Palmer's Colorado Coal & Iron Company, and with the two founded the Colorado Fuel & Iron Company, now headquartered in Pueblo. In 1903 Rockefeller, Gould, and other Eastern capitalists set

John C. Osgood

out to acquire the CF&I, and Osgood could not buck these financial titans; and control of the company passed out of his hands.

He had his coal empire for just ten years. But in that time he set into motion an entirely new concept of employer-employee relations. He envisioned an ideal industrial community, and he chose to implement that vision at Redstone, "The Ruby of the Rockies." He built attractive frame cottages for the men who worked in the coal mines 12 miles away and at the coke ovens across the river. Each cottage along the tree-shaded streets was distinctively designed and decorated. To further enhance these differences the miners, most of them immigrants, and proud of their neat homes, added their own touches reminiscent of their European homelands.

For the community Osgood built a library, a theater, an inn for bachelors, and a clubhouse. These buildings and the cottages were as modern in conveniences as city homes of the time (just before the turn of the century). The men could stop at the club and wash up and change their grimy clothes before going home. A no-treating rule operated in the club so that no one could drink himself under the table by buying drinks for someone else and having, therefore, to down another himself. This and other rules were printed in three languages, English, Italian, and Slavonic. Manual training and technical instruction were provided. Gardening and beautification were encouraged. A herd of cows was

51

Cleveholm, John C. Osgood's mansion on the Crystal River, built and furnished in 1900. At the time, Osgood owned the Colorado Fuel and Iron Co.

Redstone's neighbor is Marble, Colorado, location of the Yule Marble Co. finishing mill. It was operated off and on until 1941. The largest shipment was a single block of marble weighing 55 tons for the Tomb of the Unknown Soldier. Also shipped was $1,000,000 of marble for the Lincoln Memorial.

tended by a herder during the day and at night returned to a common barn where each owner could care for and milk his cow.

Osgood's idea of benevolent industrialism was semi-feudal in practice. Even his 42-room manor-house, Cleveholm, is reminiscent of a Tudor castle on feudal lands. No expense was spared in decorating and furnishing it. Hand-tooled green leather-and-elephant-hide covered the walls of the library, giving the room a dark richness; the music room was done in green silk brocade; the dining room in ruby velvet. Dominating the drawing room was an enormous hand-cut stone fireplace. Mrs. Osgood, who presided over this elegant domain, was affectionately called *Lady Bountiful* by the villagers. At Christmas-time all the letters to Santa Claus were brought to her, and she took delight in seeing that every child received what he wanted.

The dream lasted but a decade. The new owners of the CF&I were not so interested in bettering the living standards of the workers as had been John C. Osgood. The ideal community deteriorated, and all is quiet and ghostly in Redstone now, except for summer tourists.

THE SAN JUANS

It takes just one glance up to the prospect holes and the mining dumps on steep hillsides to realize that difficult and seemingly impossible terrain didn't deter determined prospectors. So it is not surprising that within a short time after the gold rush to the Rockies began, men should cross them and continue their search for valuable minerals in the rugged San Juans on the western slope.

Winters were harsh. People froze to death. Many were buried under the snowslides that thundered down the almost perpendicular precipices with frightening regularity. One can understand why the miners named one steep, narrow gorge *Savage Basin* and one of the mines *The Terrible*.

Despite the difficulties and terrors imposed by Nature, mines were located and poured out untold riches, and towns boomed.

Early in the '70s, two brothers paid $50,000 to a New York spiritualist for her aid in locating a mine in the West. She consulted her spirit-world contact, then pointed to a spot on the map which turned out to be King Solomon Mountain near Silverton. The brothers came to the San Juans, located what seemed to be the spirit-designated spot, and staked a claim which they named the *Highland Mary*. The medium regularly mailed instructions for digging, and the tunnels twisted and turned erratically. Several good silver veins were cut, but it was gold the brothers were after and they kept on digging. They didn't lose hope until they had spent nearly a million dollars and their funds were exhausted. They went into bankruptcy and new owners bought the mine in 1885. Using mining methods directed by engineers and geologists rather than ghosts, they made the Highland Mary one of the best producers in the region.

Although these brothers had been disdainful of silver, it was that metal that produced *the treasure of the San Juans*. One of the early prospectors declared he didn't see much gold, but there was *silver by the ton*. There was no question after that as to the name of the new camp just a-building.

53

Telluride, Colorado.

Main Street, Creede, Colorado.

* * * * *

Nicholas C. Creede, an old-time prospector disgusted with fruitless digging, paused for lunch one day in 1890 near Wagon Wheel Gap close to the headwaters of the Rio Grande, slammed his pick into the ground, looked in amazement at the dirt it kicked up, and hollered, "Holy Moses, I've struck it rich!" Sure 'nuff, the *Holy Moses* turned out to be one of the big ones. However, the stampede that usually followed rich strikes didn't really get rolling until David Moffat, president of the D&RG, purchased the claim for $70,000. Then, in no time at all a new town, named Creede, squeezed itself into a narrow canyon. Big freight wagons lumbered in bringing the things a town needs—furniture, tools, provisions, kegs of beer. The D&RG lost no time in extending its rails to the new boom town. In a few months, 10,000 people—prospectors, miners, crusaders, gamblers, merchants, women, children—were scrambling toward Creede, looking hopefully for a rich claim, or just for a place to sleep. Sleeping accommodations never could catch up with the fortune-seekers streaming in to any of the boom towns.

Nicholas C. Creede

No sooner had Creede boomed than real estate soared. A man had to start building on his lot the day he bought it, or someone else would grab it by nightfall. Houses were built wherever they could be crammed into the narrow gulch—on stilts over the stream, set precariously on the steep hillside, crowded along the one long street that was "rather straighter than a corkscrew." New residential sections were given fancy names. Every body knew that *Zephyr Glen* was really *Windy Gulch. Capitol Hill* was the mesa against which the lower town crowded.

Big underworld names cropped up in Creede from the start—Jesse James, Bob Ford, Soapy Smith. Soapy got his apprenticeship to crime in Leadville, where he cleaned the suckers with Sapolion Soap. His con game was to wrap some bars in paper money, auction them off, and the purchaser could keep any bill he found. Trouble was, only Soapy's flunkeys seemed to get those value-wrapped bars of soap. By the time he arrived in Creede, Soapy was a big shot, and was soon king of the underworld, getting cuts from every gambling concession and big deal.

All was not bad in Creede. Cy Warman, who became famous as *The Poet of the Rockies,* published a fine newspaper, the *Creede Chronicle,* in the roaring camp. When the first baby was born the town burst with pride. The father was given two suits of clothes, the mother a monster bonnet on which drifted a foot-long ostrich plume, and the family was installed in a "palatial residence" on Capitol Hill. The whole town deliberated for three days over what to name the baby girl. Then someone suggested Creede Amethyst McDonald. Amethyst was the name of another of Mr. Creede's claims. Mr. Creede was pleasantly flattered, and gave the baby the Daisy Mine, plus $100 for clothes.

Bicycling was popular among the ladies, who wore "baggy continuations," better known as bloomers, as they rode about astride their wheels. One husband was so embarrassed to see his wife in such an outfit that he ordered her to keep right on pedaling—clear back to Illinois!

* * * * *

The San Juan towns had their quota of entertainments, either brought in by professionals from the East or provided by their own ingenuity. Silverton went all out for the Scotch in 1897 with a program honoring the poet Robert Burns, the purpose being to raise money for the school library fund. The performers wore kilts; and the Silverton Weekly Miner reported "We have been told that the sensibilities of some were lacerated because certain performers appeared with bare knees. Such assumed modesty is characteristic of hypocrites. . . . The boys personally informed us that they all washed their legs before the performance, and suffered severe colds as a result." The promoters made $100 to aid the library.

In 1877, Susan B. Anthony spoke to a large gathering in Lake City on Woman's Suffrage. There were even some women among the listeners, a fact remarkable enough to be noted with interest by the male reporters who covered the event. The next year a Mr. Harbottle of New York gave a dramatic recitation of Shakespeare's King Henry V, assuming the speaking parts of 40 different characters. Admission to this virtuoso performance was 50¢.

Creede had its amusement palace, the Collins Opera House. In 1910 a traveling company presented *When Women Rule, or A.D. 2011*. Women's Lib, take note.

* * * * *

A 19-year-old Irishman from County Tipperary, who crossed the Atlantic steerage-class, became one of the mightiest of Colorado mining kings and went farther than any other in the social and international world. His name was Thomas Walsh.

Tom was a carpenter by trade and spent his first years in the U.S. building bridges. But the prospecting bug bit him hard and he tried to find quick riches in the Black Hills of South Dakota. By 1878 he was in Leadville and made some money out of a few mining claims, but more through ownership of the Grand Hotel. The important thing that happened to him here, however, was his marriage to Carrie Bell Reed. Carrie was a school teacher who had developed a beautiful figure and regal carriage by walking about her house when she was growing up balancing a glass of water on her head. So gracefully did she glide that she seemed to be rolling on coasters rather than walking. As it turned out, this was excellent preparation for her later role as a Queen of Society. The first home Tom and Carrie had was a boxcar set on logs in Sowbelly Gulch—which Carrie lost no time in re-naming *St. Keven's*—in Leadville. The silver crash of 1893 wiped out just about everything Tom had accumulated, and the family—Tom, Carrie, Evalyn, Vinson—left for Ouray in the San Juans.

There had been a lot of silver activity in this area, but it was all knocked into oblivion by the silver crash, and most of the mines had been abandoned. Tom began to explore the old tunnels and dumps, and became convinced there was gold still to be taken out of these mountains. He bought up claims for a song. In 1896 he walked into the tunnel of one of his newly-acquired claims, the Camp Bird (so-named because a camp bird, also called Camp Robbers and Whiskey Jacks, had eaten the lunch of the original prospector). Tom came to a three-foot vein of quartz

Thomas Walsh

which he recognized as gold in tellurium form. Since no shining metal showed, previous miners, looking for silver-lead carbonates, had passed this vein by as being valueless. Carrie happened to be in Denver at the time, and Tom, needing to share his exciting discovery with someone, yet needing even more to keep it secret, confided to 10-year-old Evalyn, "Daughter, I've struck it rich!" while warning her to say not a word to a soul. He quickly bought up surrounding claims, then began to develop the Camp Bird. The first profits went right back into development. He built a smelter and a two-mile tram to bring down the ores from the mine. For the miners he constructed a fine boarding house, three stories high, with hardwood floors, reading rooms, porcelain bathtubs, marble-topped lavatories, hot and cold water, and electric lights.

By 1900 the Camp Bird properties included 103 mining claims which were producing between $3,000,000 and $4,000,000 annually. The Camp Bird, with its six-mile vein of gold, became one of the largest and most productive gold mines in the world, and second in the United States only to the Portland in Cripple Creek.

A train wreck which took several lives but in which the Walsh family fortunately suffered only a few bruises, plus several other close calls on treacherous mountain roads, made the Walshes decide to leave Ouray and move to Washington, D.C., where living would be less risky. With Tom's outgoing friendliness and money, and Carrie's charm, the Walshes were soon leaders in Washington's society, hob-nobbing with the great and the famous in politics, society, the arts. President McKinley appointed Tom a Commissioner to the Paris Exposition and the family sailed for Europe. Here, King Leopold of Belgium courted Tom's friendship—he hoped to form a partnership with him to develop mining in the Belgian Congo. (Harum-scarum 14-year-old Evalyn thought the King looked unnaturally stiff, as though he were wearing a corset, and she purposely bumped into him to feel for herself. It was more than a corset—it was a long solid bullet-proof garment.)

In 1902 John Hays Hammond persuaded Tom to sell the Camp Bird to a London Syndicate for $5,200,000. In the years that followed, the Syndicate got back several times that amount.

Camp Bird Mine

Power Plant at the top of Bridal Veil Falls, Telluride.

58

Tom built a million-dollar, 60-room mansion in Washington, at 2020 Massachusetts Avenue, that became the social, international, and political center of the city. Everyone whose name appears in governmental annals or Society's "400" was entertained at "2020" in a succession of elaborate dinners, formal receptions, elegant soirees. Evalyn married Ned McLean, son of the owner of the Washington Post and the Cincinnati Enquirer, and thus two multi-million dollar fortunes were joined.

Tom died in 1910; Carrie lived another quarter-century. Their daughter Evalyn Walsh McLean continued to make social history and headlines until her death in 1947. She had always had a passion for jewels. When she eloped with Ned McLean, her father told her to buy herself a wedding present. She did—the 92½ carat *Star of the East* diamond, for $120,000. A few years after Tom's death she bought one of the rarest and most famous jewels in the world, the blue Hope diamond.

The legendary history of this jewel tells that Louis XIV of France had his agent purchase a 112½ carat crudely-cut diamond in India, and had it recut into a heart-shaped 67-carat stone. It almost certainly adorned the person of the famous Madame de Maintenon. Louis XVI inherited it, and it must have been worn by the tragic Marie Antoinette. After being owned by several other royal personages, it came into possession of Henry Philip Hope, an English gem collector, who gave it his name. Eventually, Evalyn McLean bought the *Hope,* now recut to a 44½ carat slightly-oval shaped stone, for $154,000.

At Mrs. McLean's death a jeweler, Harry Winston, bought her gem collection, including the Hope, for $1.1 million. In 1958 he offered it to the Smithsonian Institute to be used as the center piece for a collection of jewels similar to the Crown Jewels in the Tower of London. He mailed it to Washington from New York, the postage being $145.29—for insurance of one million dollars.

In her story of her father's (and her own) life, *Father Struck It Rich*—the phrase he had used to tell 10-year-old Evalyn of his breathtaking strike at the Camp Bird—Tom Walsh's daughter makes it inescapably clear that wealth does not bring health or happiness or freedom from tragedy. Her son was killed by a car; a daughter died of an overdose of sleeping pills; her granddaughter and namesake died from alcohol-barbiturate poisoning; her husband drank himself into insanity. It seemed that the Hope diamond, so rare, so lovely, carried in its incredible blue brilliance a mysterious curse.

*　　*　　*　　*　　*

A famous contest of the turn of the century—*The Battle of the Currents*—had its climax in Telluride. The "Battle" raged between two electrical geniuses, Thomas A. Edison and Nikola Tesla.

Edison's experiments led to direct current, which required a power-house every square mile. Tesla's discovery, alternating current, on the other hand, made it possible, by using transformers, to carry much more electricity much farther distances, on the same size wire—a system that was to revolutionize power distribution and make possible the electronic world of today.

Tesla had come to the United States from his native Slavia in the early '90s, and rented a New York laboratory in which to conduct his electrical experiments. By the end of the decade he had reached the limit in which high voltages could be handled within a city building. Sparks jumped to walls, floor, ceiling. At this crucial point he was invited to locate his laboratory in Colorado Springs, and was promised plenty of space and all the electric power he needed. Furthermore, he would be on hand to study the violent electrical storms that broke on summer afternoons.

Another electrical inventor, George Westinghouse, had been right in the middle of the *Battle of the Currents,* and had become convinced that Tesla's alternating current provided the practical solution to electrical problems. But it had never been tested in the field. Over in Telluride, Colorado, high-altitude mines were facing bankruptcy because of the cost of fuel to provide steam power for their operations. Someone asked Westinghouse if he could find some means of creating cheap power. He studied the San Miguel River, which falls 500 feet in less than a mile, and came up with what he hoped would be a solution. He built a dam at the top of the cascades and a power plant in the valley below. Then, using machinery designed on Tesla's patents, Westinghouse made the first practical and successful application of alternating current.

Arthur Brisbane, noted editor, gave an evaluation of the scientific and electrical genius, Nikola Tesla "He is thin, and has very big hands. His thumbs are remarkably big. This is a good sign—the apes have very small thumbs. . . . Tesla lives his life up in the top of his head, where ideas are born."

Tesla was a resident of Colorado only briefly; but he deserves a place among the Centennial State's colorful characters because his work done and tested here had, perhaps, a larger and more far-reaching impact on the world of the future than that of any other.

* * * *

In the late fall of 1873 a group of Utah prospectors, with Alferd Packer as guide, came into the San Juans. The winter was severe. Come spring, and Packer limped into the Los Piños Indian Agency, alone. How had he stayed alive? By eating his companions! Oh, Packer had quite another story, but evidence mounted that this was what had actually happened. The sheriff put chains on Packer, but he escaped, and it was nine years before the law caught up with him again. This time there was a famous, and controversial, trial, the only cannibalism trial ever held in the U.S., and Packer received a stiff sentence.

Three years he spent in the Gunnison jail, during which time the sheriff is said to have told a group of rioting inmates to shut up and get back in their cells or he'd turn Packer loose on them! The *man-eater,* as people had begun calling Packer, was transferred to the State Pen at Canon City, where he stayed for 15 years, until he was paroled in 1901.

The Packer affair had, we might say, political overtones. After the trial, Larry Dolan, a barkeeper, shouted words that have been quoted again and again: "They're gonna hang Packer! The jedge, he says, 'Stand up, y' man-eatin' son-iv-a — — —.'" Then, pintin' his finger at him, so ragin' mad wuz he, he says, 'They wuz sivin Dimmycrats in Hinsdale County, and yez ate foive iv them. Damn ye! I sintins ye t' be hanged 'til yez are dead, dead, dead, as a warnin' ag'in reducin' th' Dimmycrat populashion iv th' state!' "

Alferd Packer

In the 1930s a group of practical jokers printed up Certificates of Membership in the Packer Club of Colorado, the stipulation for membership being a promise to eliminate five "Nu Deal Dimmycrats."

About the same time, Packer was "absolved" of his crime. He had died in 1907, and was buried in the Littleton cemetery. A colorful Denver character, Frank Hamilton Rice, bishop of the "Liberal Church" which he founded, went out to the cemetery in the dead of night with six black-robed men and, quoting Bible verses that condone cannibalism (one example Leviticus 26:29, which reads, "Ye shall eat the flesh of your sons, and the flesh of your daughters ye shall eat") he "absolved Packer of the crime of cannibalism."

So endeth the story of Alferd Packer. Some historians spell his name *Alfred;* however, the following would seem to prove *Alferd* correct. In May, 1883, formal printed invitations were issued "to attend the

** EXECUTION OF ALFERD PACKER **
At Lake City, Colorado
On the 19th day of May, A.D. 1883
(Signed) Clair Smith,
Sheriff of Hinsdale Co., Colo."

(As noted, he got off with a prison sentence, not execution.)

IV.

THE SKY PILOTS

" We will provoke each other
to love and good works "

Frequently in the early days ardent preachers, bent on saving the miners from their mortal sins, arrived in the roaring mining camps on the same rattling stagecoaches that brought the embodiment of those sins, *Les Girls* themselves. While the women set up their fancy parlor houses, the sky-pilots preached hell-fire and damnation in streets, saloons, wherever they could gather an audience.

One of the first to come was Big John Chivington, later to gain questionable fame as the commander of the militia at the Sand Creek Massacre (see Chapter I, *Indians on the Warpath*). A Methodist, Chivington was sent to Colorado Territory as Presiding Elder in 1860. On Sunday mornings, he would stride into a saloon and order the bartender to clear the shelves of whiskey bottles, lay the pistols he always carried on the pulpit (a table or perhaps a whiskey keg), and preach to whoever would listen.

Chivington was not the only one to preach in saloons. Over in Creede, an itinerant preacher delivered his sermon standing on a pool table, using a faro table as his altar. That night someone stole his pants, and Soapy Smith, underworld boss, caught up with the thief and made him return them—after forcing him to add a sizable contribution to the money he found in the pockets.

At the close of these impromptu worship services, the prospectors, miners, gamblers, prostitutes usually joined together in repeating the Lord's Prayer.

Money was hard to come by. On one two-month, 500-mile trek, Father John L. Dyer collected all of $43. Father Dyer was also a Methodist, though he was a layman, not an ordained minister. He had been converted at a Methodist camp meeting and his call as a man of God was so strong, even without ordination, that he felt compelled to preach. He spoke from the pulpit of many a midwestern church. Then it was 1859,

the Colorado gold rush was on, and, like everybody else, Father Dyer's thoughts turned westward. Though he had but $15 to his name, he determined to take the gospel to the prospectors and miners in the roaring mountain camps.

The last night out before reaching Denver, someone stole his last two dollars and a-half. But, philosophized John Dyer, "I was consoled in the fact that I was no worse off than I would have been if it had been five thousand dollars."

Father Dyer was the first to preach in many a Colorado mining camp. If he couldn't find a building, he had his "congregation" sit on logs out in the open. Collections were scanty, and Father Dyer eked out his existence by becoming a mailman, express-agent, newspaper salesman, part-time

Father Dyer

prospector. When winter came, he made himself a pair of snowshoes, 11 feet long, and forever after he was known as *The Snowshoe Itinerant*. Every now and then Father Dyer came into competition with Father Joseph Macheboeuf and Reverend Sheldon Jackson, who were

founding Catholic and Presbyterian churches as zealously as Dyer was founding Methodist ones. But the Methodist simply quoted St. Paul, "We will provoke each other to love and good works"—and that's just what they did.

Father Macheboeuf was such an active, hardworking saint that Willa Cather took him as the model for Father Joseph Vaillant in her book, *Death Comes for the Archbishop*. Before becoming Bishop of Denver he had established Catholic communities over a large part of the Rockies, bumping over the trails in a little square buggy containing a portable altar. One day in 1863, near Central City, he met a train of heavily-laden ore wagons on a narrow shelf road, and in squeezing to the outside to let them pass, his little cart tipped over and he was

Father Macheboeuf

thrown out on the rocks. His leg was badly broken and was not properly set, and he limped badly and painfully the rest of his life.

Father Macheboeuf was short and slight, his skin hardened and seamed by exposure to bitter weather, his graying hair sunburn-streaked

—altogether a homely man. But in his poorly-built body was the driving power of a dozen men, and he kept up a time-and-distance schedule that would have worn all of them out. He bolstered his morale and stamina and enthusiasm daily by offering up a morning prayer: "I thank God that I have more work than I can do."

The Presbyterians were not about to be left out of the missionary field that opened up with the mining era. Reverend Sheldon Jackson's path crossed those of Father Macheboeuf and the *Snowshoe Itinerant* frequently. Reverend Jackson was born in New York in 1834, and as a baby his parents dedicated him to the service of God; neither he nor they ever questioned his calling. As he matured, his interest in education almost caught up with his passion for religion; in the end it surpassed it.

Rev. Sheldon Jackson

After his ordination he was sent to the west with the earliest tide of pioneers to take charge of all Presbyterian mission work from Mexico to Canada and from Nebraska to Nevada. Always ahead of the game, he posted notices along the trail: "Presbyterians moving west will please leave their names and destination with the Reverend Sheldon Jackson, so that they may be looked after and church privileges supplied them as early as possible.' Only one Presbyterian registered; but that didn't deter the peripatetic clergyman from his appointed task of organizing and overseeing new churches. He firmly believed, "Where two or three are gathered together. . . ." However, it didn't always work out. The only Presbyterian in one small community wasn't interested; he said he didn't want to be organized.

The story is told that, as Reverend Jackson looked toward the vast uninhabited area ahead of him, he fell on his knees to pray for divine help and strength in his enormous task; and that, rising, he spread wide his arms and proclaimed: "I claim this and all beyond for the Presbyterian Church." And this is the title of one brief biography of the preacher who was called "the biggest little man in America": *The Bishop of All Beyond*.

From the first, Reverend Jackson was an ardent advocate of education, both for settlers and Indians. When a new undeveloped territory opened up with the purchase of Alaska from the Russians, the Mission Board sent him, in 1877, to that cold North country to repeat his endeavors among the Eskimos and the incoming settlers. The government in Washington, recognizing his abilities, appointed him General Agent for Education in Alaska.

Small of stature, large of heart, fervent of spirit, the Reverend Sheldon Jackson left his personal imprint on as vast an area as any one man in America.

Permission to use material from *The Bishop of All Beyond,* published by Friendship Press, New York, in 1948, personally granted by the author, Winifred E. Hulbert, who completed preliminary work on the book by Mary Jenness.

* * * * *

As soon as families began to join the men in a pioneer community, church groups were formed, and in a short time churches reminiscent of those in New England and mid-America were going up. The lonely women, far from childhood homes, in a harsh new environment, wanted a touch of the quiet, the familiar, the loved and sorely-missed. So it is understandable why most of the tiny early churches looked like they might have been transplanted right out of the gentle setting of the East into the rugged mountains of the West. The little white-steepled churches fit in well with the Victorian gingerbread architecture of many of the small homes in the mining towns, and both contrast sharply with the stark shafts and tipples of the mines so close by.

Problems sometimes presented themselves when new churches were started. In more than one community the site had to be guarded to ward off claim jumpers. The miners, not notably religious types, frequently gave generously toward the building of the churches. In one case, a donor was consulted concerning the purchase of a chandelier, but he vetoed it as an unnecessary expense, saying, "Nobody knows how to play it anyhow."

Buryin' was a frequent service required of the Men of God. Life was hard, death always sad, sometimes violent. Necktie parties were no novelty. He who hung from a tree did truly receive a suspended sentence, and he certainly died of a stoppage of the breath. There was a corpse to be buried, and the preachers performed the last rites over the bad guys as well as the good.

Cemeteries in the old mining towns are interesting, if mournful, places to visit. Graves of old-timers are historical documents in themselves. The number of children's graves, sometimes four or five of a family who died within months of each other, are mute and touching testimony to the ravages of diphtheria, pneumonia, children's diseases, in an era lacking protective or curative drugs, and in homes far from medical help. Bereft parents poured out their grief in such lines as:

"We just began to view thy bloom,
When thou wert called away."

"Earth has one pure spirit less —
Heaven one inmate more."

"Budded on earth,
Blossomed in heaven."

The Men of God were always there to give comfort in these times of sorrow. They were truly men who stood a mile tall.

Presbyterian Church, Golden, Colorado. One of the first churches founded by Sheldon Jackson, built in 1870.

The town of Irwin was platted in 1879 and survived but a brief 5 years. In spite of the short span of life, its Main Street features a church of substantial size.

V

THE EMPIRE BUILDERS

"   *.......Indians......threw themselves in terror*
upon the trembling earth as the great
black steed .... roared by "

or all the mineral riches stored in its mountains, and the agricultural bonanzas lying dormant in its plains waiting to be brought to life by irrigation, Colorado could not have developed to its full potential had it not been for the railroads. The men who brought the shining rails across the plains, over the passes, and through the tunnels were the real empire builders.

David H. Moffat was the first to reach Colorado Territory. On March 21, 1860, the Rocky Mountain News of Denver carried the following item:

"On Saturday, 17th, D. H. Moffat and W. M. Keith [arrived], 29 days from Omaha, three men and two teams, freighted with books and stationery, to establish a store in this city."

The tall, thin young man, Moffat, weighing a slight hundred pounds, looked as though the strong winds might blow him away. But strength and stamina were in his thin body, and capabilities and ambition. These qualities were to carry him to the very top in wealth, position, and influence in Colorado.

His education had been in a country school in the little village of Washingtonville, New York. While still a lad, he left home to make his way in the world, went to New York City, and became a bank messenger, quickly rising to the position of assistant teller. By the time he was 17 he was sent to Omaha to become cashier of the Bank of Nebraska. There he met a merchant who was looking for a young man to open a book and stationery store in Denver, and

David H. Moffat

the two formed a partnership. Moffat was 21 when he arrived in Denver. A few years later he was back in the banking business, as cashier of the First National Bank of Denver, and was on his way to becoming the financial, mining, and railroad czar of Colorado.

Early day Denver, 16th and Arapahoe Sts., in the mid-1880's. This was about the time that Moffat became president of the Denver & Rio Grande.

The Moffat Tunnel, finished in 1928, 12 years after Moffat died. Moffats' dream was a transcontinental main-line through Denver, a possibility only if an economical way was found to cross the divide. The Moffat Tunnel was the answer.

The bank had been established in 1865 with Jerome B. Chaffee as president. Chaffee had made his first fortune in the Bobtail Mine at Central City. With Chaffee, Moffat was to become a mining magnate. They bought the rich Caribou mine (which furnished the silver bricks for President Grant to walk on in Central City); a half interest in Tabor's *Little Pittsburg* in Leadville (and Tabor, in reciprocation, bought a half interest in the First National Bank); and some 100 other mines.

Following the Civil War, Moffat and other Colorado business leaders redoubled their efforts to bring a transcontinental railroad through the Territory to Denver. They were sure the Union Pacific would pass through the city with its main line. But it was not to be; the surveyors chose a route westward from Cheyenne, Wyoming, where the mountain passes were lower. Then came word that a Union Pacific vice-president had remarked that Denver "was too dead to bury." Those were fighting words. Immediately plans were made to build a connecting line between Denver and Cheyenne, and on June 15, 1868, the first engine, bearing the name of David H. Moffat, rolled into Denver. Moffat continued to build short intra-state railroads to strategic mining areas; he persuaded Otto Mears to build railroads in the San Juans; in 1887 he became president of General Palmer's Denver & Rio Grande.

Jerome B. Chaffee

David Moffat played a major role in every phase of Colorado's early life, mining, railroading, business and industry, finance, politics. His friendliness and generosity were legendary, and he was always ready to hold out a helping hand.

Still his dream was unfulfilled — his dream of a railroad tunnel through the mountains. Still Denver sat at the base of the great mountain barrier, its cross-country travelers having to detour to continue west. Due west from Denver were only high mountain passes and the rocky trails over which big freight wagons creaked and groaned and rattled. For 44 years Moffat dreamed of a tunnel that would carry the rails westward from Denver under the Continental Divide; for years survey teams measured and probed for the best and shortest route to cut through.

Empire-Builder Moffat was 63 when, at long last, he saw "the light at the end of the tunnel," if not in reality, then in feasibility. In 1911, with the dream seemingly close to fulfilment, he died. It was 12 years, however, before the famed Moffat Tunnel was finally begun. In 1928 the first train rolled through; in June, 1934, all connecting tracks completed, the first through passenger train from Denver to Salt Lake City roared into the East Portal and came out six miles beyond, at Winter Park, cutting off 175 miles between the two cities.

David Moffat's dream had finally become a reality.

Like many another Civil War veteran, General William Jackson Palmer, one of the youngest generals in the Union Army, reasoned that the West, just opening up, offered great challenges and opportunities. From age 17 until he joined the army eight years later, he had worked in railroading, becoming confidential secretary to the president of the Pennsylvania Railroad; so it was natural that, when hostilities ceased, he again went into railroading.

In 1869 he was engaged by the Kansas Pacific to survey routes through Colorado Territory to Denver. He became convinced that the road should border the Arkansas to Pueblo and then turn north along the Front Range to Denver, thereby securing the trade from the fertile Arkansas Valley as well as from Pueblo, a rising industrial center. The decision was made, however, to bring the road toward Denver over the most direct route from Kansas—through settlements with such picturesque names as Eagle Tail, Monotony, First View, Wild Horse, Mirage —and General Palmer began construction.

Gen. William Jackson Palmer

Contracts were let for grading, for construction of bridges and culverts, for the cutting of ties. To get the ties, used at the rate of 2500 to the mile, the General hired 700 ox and 100 mule teams.

When work crews heading both east and west came within 10¼ miles of each other, a flag was placed in the middle of the gap so that each side had 5⅛ miles to go in a race to capture the flag. Work commenced at 5 o'clock on the morning of August 15, 1870; ten hours later the rails met. This record — 10¼ miles in 10 hours — surpassed anything in the history of railroad building. A thousand people had been invited to come out from Denver by special train to watch the closing of the gap. On their return to the city the whole party was entertained by General Palmer at dinner. Among the guests was Dr. William A. Bell. The young Englishman had been in St. Louis to study homeopathy when he heard of General Palmer's survey party, and he determined to join it. The only vacancy was for a photographer, but that didn't stop Dr. Bell. He took a crash course in the primitive and complicated photographic process of that time, and, armed with these hurriedly-acquired skills, he applied and was accepted. Dr. Bell was to become General Palmer's associate in all his later ventures.

All during the time he was building the Kansas-Pacific, the General had in the back of his mind the idea of constructing a railroad of his own to border the Front Range southward from Denver. His road would be a personal venture, under his own control, with his friends associated with him in its management and operation. On October 27, 1870, the Denver and Rio Grande was incorporated with capital stock of $2,500,000.

Chairman of the Board of Directors was William P. Mellen of New York, and it was Mr. Mellen's daughter Queen whom General Palmer married.

Surveys were made of the proposed route and when the survey team reached Colorado City, a tiny settlement at the base of Pikes Peak, one member remarked that the junction of Monument and Fountain Creeks opposite the entrance to Ute Pass would be an excellent site for an important town on the railroad. This seed touched fertile ground in the General's mind and he began acquisition of some 10,500 surrounding acres. By buying up Agricultural College Scrip at 80¢ an acre, he acquired the land for less than $10,000.

Construction of the railroad began in January 1871; in July a group forming the Colorado Springs Company came to the chosen spot to drive the first stake, lay out a town, appraise the lots, and start business; and in Ocober the first tiny train, crowded with special guests, speeded southward from Denver over the first 76 miles of completed narrow-gauge track, at the astonishing rate of 15 miles an hour, to the site of the new city.

Laying of the tracks continued toward Pueblo, and on April 27, 1872, that city had its first railroad. In 1874, the rails reached Canon City, but there being little on the upper Arkansas at that time to justify construction of a railroad westward, the company devoted its resources to continuing south from Pueblo. Depression and panic in the financial world caused delay after delay, and it was not until April 1876 that the railroad approached Trinidad. Then, to the anger of the people of that city, the railroad stopped at El Moro, five miles away on the Purgatoire River, but in plain view of the older city. A cardinal aim of the D&RG was the creation of new towns.

In the meantime, the Santa Fe had been heading westward slowly. The Gazette of Colorado Springs opined that the road would have been completed long since if General Palmer and his narrow gauge boys had been in charge. It was March, 1876, when the Santa Fe pulled into Pueblo and met the D&RG which had arrived four years earlier.

The original plan of the D&RG was to continue the railroad over Raton Pass to El Paso, Texas, and eventually to Mexico City. In February, 1878, a construction crew left Pueblo for El Moro to begin work on the Raton Pass section. A few hours later, the Santa Fe, which had been keeping a wary eye on D&RG activities, chartered a special train—to run over D&RG rails—to take its own crews to Raton Pass.

The special passed the regular train which carried the D&RG crew, and reached El Moro at 11 p.m. The foreman rushed his men to the Pass and started them to work. When the Rio Grande crew arrived the next morning, they found their rivals already on the job. The D&RG withdrew, leaving the Santa Fe in possession of the southward route.

The D&RG centered its energies now on getting over La Veta Pass. At one point of the tortuous route, to cover a half mile it was necessary to build 2½ miles of track, trestle, embankment, wye; at another, a horseshoe curve measured two miles around, but was only 750 feet from point to point, with the upper curve 400 feet above the lower. It was said that

71

General Palmers baby railroad near the summit of La Veta Pass. The term "baby" came from the narrowness of gauge, 3 feet wide tracks instead of the standard gauge of 4 feet 8½ inches.

In 1881, Palmer's D&RG narrow gauge had reached Durango. Part of this trackage still survives—the Silverton extension and the portion over Cumbres Pass, where this picture was taken in 1952. Tourist runs are still made over these areas in the summer.

a narrow gauge line "could curve on the brim of a sombrero," and General Palmer's *baby railroad* almost proved it.

In 1877 Leadville started booming, and the Santa Fe made moves to secure a right-of-way through the Royal Gorge to the upper Arkansas, and planned to begin work in the spring of 1878. At the same time, the D&RG decided to push through the Gorge, which it had foresightedly surveyed and staked several years before. Again the Santa Fe tried to charter a special over D&RG tracks, but having been stung once, the Rio Grande refused. The Santa Fe ordered W. R. Morley to proceed to Canon City by one means or another, and he secured a horse and galloped out to try to overtake the D&RG work train. The horse collapsed, but Mr. Morley rushed on by foot to the entrance to the canyon and was diligently digging when the Rio Grande men arrived. That is, according to one story. Another had the Rio Grande crew there first, by half an hour, to validate its claim to the Gorge. The *Royal Gorge War* that followed was a battle royal, though bloodless. Men of one camp laid rails by day and tore up those of their rivals by night; stones were rolled from the top of the gorge; bridges were burned; stone "forts" were constructed; employees were lured from one line to the other by offers of higher pay or shorter hours. Guns were brandished, but fortunately no lives were lost.

The Royal Gorge War was a crisis point in a two-year-long legal battle between the two railroads. Lawsuits, claims, counter-claims, injunctions were filed and brought to court. Decisions were made, then reversed. Trains carried guards and armed men were stationed at the depots. Telegraph wires were cut; sheriffs and attorneys were bribed; an attempt was made to kidnap the judge. The whole matter ended in a compromise in April, 1880: The D&RG would have total rights to the track through the Gorge; the two companies would divide the states of Colorado and New Mexico between them as far as further railroad expansion was concerned.

With the railroad "war" over, the valiant little D&RG rushed headlong to tap the riches of the latest mining fields, reaching Leadville in 1880 and Durango in the San Juans in 1881. Durango was another of General Palmer's railroad-created towns, this time depriving Animas City of the prize.

Unfortunately, loss of revenue during the two years of litigation, and high costs of construction in rugged terrain, forced the General to share his little road with others. One of them was Jay Gould, the shrewd exploiter of railroads in financial difficulties, and to him the General sadly turned over control of his Rio Grande. Gould and other eastern capitalists had become interested in the D&RG because it was a narrow gauge road for which construction costs were lower and which, it was felt, was the best kind of road for the mountains.

By 1887 narrow gauge had lost favor, even though a third rail had been added to the tracks so that standard gauge engines could pull narrow gauge cars. When David H. Moffat acquired the railroad from Gould, he set about immediately converting it to standard gauge.

Back in 1875, when the D&RG was contemplating various routes into New Mexico, the citizens of Socorro had adopted a resolution pledging their assistance in building the railroad to their town. It read in part:

Early view of downtown Colorado Springs, approximately 1880, from Pikes Peak Avenue, with the famous peak in the background.

General Palmer's residence, Glen Eyrie, in the Garden of the Gods, Colorado Springs. (This is the original home around which the present-day "Castle" was built.)

"Be it resolved that we believe the *Baby Railroad,* called the Denver and Rio Grande Narrow Gauge . . . will be of great benefit to the territory, and that Governor Hunt and General Palmer, who . . . with so much credit to themselves are managing the road, have our best wishes and sincere sympathy."

The General was to learn the hard way that he needed more than "best wishes and sincere sympathy" to run a railroad in competition with the ruthless East-West giants.

In planning his ideal city, Colorado Springs, the General was a visionary and an idealist, but a practical, far-sighted realist, too. The city would be *a place for homes, for schools, for science—the most attractive place for residence in the entire West.* There would be wide streets, space for parks, grounds for a college. He planted hundreds of trees on the grassy plain.

He was determined to make his city a cultural oasis in the wild west, and he succeeded. The magnificent mountain setting and the bright sunshine brought wealthy tourists as well as settlers, and before long Colorado Springs was known as the *Newport of the Rockies.* Many English people came, some of them because they had invested in the D&RG through Dr. Bell's solicitation, and Colorado Springs gained added renown as *Little London.* The British flag was flown on Queen Victoria's birthday, and policemen were called *Bobbies.*

The pure air and healthful climate attracted health seekers, and many of them regained their health and stayed to become leaders in business and society.

General and Mrs. Palmer had three daughters, and Queen took the girls to England and gave them an English education. After her death, when she was only 44, the girls came home to Colorado Springs, and the General built for them a stone, castle-like mansion near the Garden of the Gods, which he called Glen Eyrie for an eagle's nest on one of the high rocks in the lovely, secluded glen.

In 1906, the General was injured when his horse stumbled and he was thrown. He was paralyzed for two years before he died. But this didn't stop General Palmer. His doctor designed a rounded, spoon-shaped, form-fitting case stuffed with hair and feathers to fit into the big White Steamer the General bought, and he continued to go wherever he wished.

Ten months after his accident, the General did one of the most magnanimous deeds of his life. The doctor refused permission for him to attend the 35th reunion of his Fifteenth Pennsylvania Cavalry, so he brought the 280 old soldiers out to Colorado Springs and gave them the time of their lives. There was a parade, led by General Palmer in a dazzling white uniform—reclining on his form-fitting seat in the White Steamer. A few months later, with a retinue of 14 nurses and servants and his physician and daughters, he made a trip to England and the Continent.

General William Jackson Palmer, a giant among early Colorado pioneers, left behind him a lasting memorial—the City of Colorado Springs. His fame, said one eulogist, would endure as long as the mountains which the rails of his Baby Railroad conquered.

A group photo of the 35th reunion of the 15th Pennsylvania Cavalry, where General Palmer brought 280 old soldiers together in Colorado Springs. He is shown, in the center, in the special form-fitting couch, dressed in his white uniform.

A little man not five feet tall was another of the giants of Colorado, another of the Empire Builders. He was Otto Mears, *Pathfinder of the San Juans*.

Mears was born in Russia in 1841 and was orphaned before he was four. The scrawny little fellow was shunted from one household to another, and finally was sent to an uncle in San Francisco. But no one was there to meet the lonely 11-year-old—the uncle had gone off to Australia. Thrown on his own, in a strange city, scarcely able to speak the language, the plucky lad got a job selling newspapers and began to support himself. For eight years he made his way doing odd jobs, and when he was 19 he set off for the Nevada mining camps.

Thoroughly American by the time the Civil War started, he joined the California Volunteers on the side of the Union and was sent to the southwest to fight the Texans who had joined the Confederacy. He ended his war service as a Captain, then served under Kit Carson in his campaign against the Navajos.

Mears liked this part of the country and decided to go into business for himself in Conejos in the San Luis Valley. Within a year he had a store, a sawmill, a grist mill, and a wheat farm. To get his products across the mountains into the Arkansas Valley and to the market in booming Leadville, he built a road over Poncha Pass, which the government allowed him to operate as a toll road. With this Mears struck his stride; from now on, road building was in his blood.

While freighting his goods to Leadville, young Otto met an attractive, auburn-haired German girl who lived in Granite, and married her in 1870. He built a combination general merchandise store and home in Saguache, and to this honeymoon cottage he brought his bride.

His second toll road, built in 1871, went west from Saguache to the present site of Lake City. It so happened that in that very year, silver and gold were discovered in the San Juans, and almost immediately his toll road became a busy and profitable thorofare. Before he himself moved to the San Juans, he had built a 300-mile network of roads in the San Luis Valley.

The Utes, for whom the San Juans had been home for generations, naturally resented the rush of white men to lands they considered their own. Otto Mears made removing the Indians to smaller reservations to the west, his first order of business, thereby opening this area to settlement. He played a prominent role in drawing up the various treaties by which the Utes lost their lands. The first was the Brunot Treaty of 1873, named for Felix Brunot, the U.S. Indian Commissioner, in which the Utes gave up their San Juan area for a payment of $25,000 a year. Mears advised Commissioner Brunot to add $1000 a year "salary" for Chief Ouray personally, and this flattered and pleased the Indian.

In 1880 Mears was asked to serve as one of five commissioners to make another treaty with the Utes. The government was prepared to pay $1,800,000 to the Indians for the balance of their land, 11,000,000 acres on the western slope. Mears had a better idea. He gave each Indian two dollars to sign the treaty, thereby saving the government practically

Toll station at Bear Creek Falls on the wagon road Mears built between Ouray and Ironton. This is now the Million Dollar Highway.

This is the first combination train on Mears' Silverton R.R., between Silverton and Red Mountain. This was the first of four railroads Mears built in Colorado. (Mears is the man standing in front of the engine.)

78

the total sum it had expected to pay. Mears was charged with bribery; but he was so convincing when he said the Indians were happier with a small cash payment now than a promised larger one later, that the case was dismissed.

Mears saw the great challenge of this land he had dickered over with the Indians. Rich in minerals, gorgeous in scenery, the area was boxed in by giant mountains. Now they were faced by a giant midget, a man to whom there was no such word as *impossible*. His experience in road-building had not been in this kind of rugged terrain, but this did not stop him; the roads he knew were necessary for development of the area speedily took shape and soon connected the major boom towns of the San Juans. Supplies and fortune-seekers came in over his roads, millions in rich ore went out.

The Silverton *Solid Muldoon* of April 13, 1883, described a portion of the road that later came to be called the Million Dollar Highway: "The wagon road . . . is dangerous even to pedestrians. . . . The average depth of the mud is three feet . . . the grade is four parts vertical and one part perpendicular."

When the Denver and Rio Grande decided to push into the San Juans, Mears was offered the seemingly impossible job of builder. Though he had never built railroads, he met the challenge. Using many of his earlier roads as bases, he lowered the grades, flattened out the curves, laid the tracks where they would be protected as much as possible from snow and rock slides, and connected the towns by narrow gauge rails. Numerous switchbacks and wyes, even a corkscrew turntable, were used to carry the rails up the steep grades and through the narrow box canyons. The *Ophir Loop* was as spectacular, if not as famous, as the Georgetown loop. Legend has it that Mears himself was so terrified when he took his first ride on the Loop that he wanted to get out and walk. (It was said that Ophir received its name when an early traveler, noticing a big cave opening on the hill, exclaimed, "O fer God's sake, lookit that hole!" More likely, it was named for the famous Ophir Mine of the Comstock Lode in Nevada, which, no doubt, had been named by someone with Biblical knowledge who named it *Ophir* for the gold region in Arabia to which Solomon sent his fleet to purchase the precious metal).

Hired as the track-builder, Mears soon owned the railroads he had built. Passes issued to prominent people were filigree-bordered rectangles of gold or silver bearing the recipient's name; less important persons received passes made of buckskin.

In 1888 Mears was appointed to the Board of Capitol Commissioners to construct the Colorado State Capitol. The cornerstone was laid July 4, 1890, the building was in use by 1896, and finally completed and dedicated in 1908. The cost was close to $3,000,000.

Otto Mears, with everything against him as a youth, became a true Empire Builder. His 91 years of life spanned the most exciting era of western development.

* * * * *

Cy Warman, *Poet of the Rockies,* described the coming of the *Iron Horse* to the West: "Some Indians fought it, but most threw themselves in terror upon the trembling earth as the great black steed with heart of fire and breath of flame, roared by. . . . The white man watched it tip over the crest of the continent, and the West of Yesterday was gone forever."

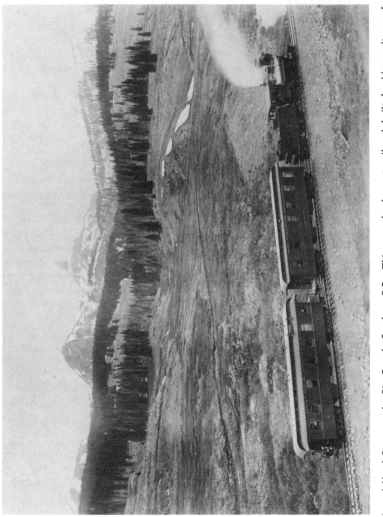

Top of Lizzard Head Pass, on the Rio Grande Southern R.R. This was the longest railroad built by Mears, it ran from Ridgeway to Durango, by Telluride. This is a Jackson photo taken in the 1870's.

VI

THE BOWL OF GOLD

" ....the world-shaking bonanza -

GOLD AT CRIPPLE CREEK!"

When the pioneers crossed the plains toward the mountains in 1859, they expected to find gold at Pikes Peak. The gold was there, all right, but these seekers didn't find it. Not for 30 years was gold discovered at Pikes Peak. By that time the city founded by General William Jackson Palmer at the eastern base of the mountain, Colorado Springs, had been thriving for 20 years. Then came the world-shaking bonanza—Gold at Cripple Creek!

During the 1880s a lone cowboy named Bob Womack searched for gold in almost every foot of the bleak, barren bowl, an extinct volcanic crater, on the west side of Pikes Peak. The area had been dubbed Cripple Creek because some cows had broken their legs scrambling down the rocky banks of a dry little creek bed. Now Bob's employers reprimanded him for making further hazards for the cattle by digging so many prospect

Bob Womack

holes. People thought Bob was plumb crazy. Why, gold was found in stream beds, where it had washed out from mother lodes of quartz in the mountains. These gently rounded hills resembled in no way the mountains that contained outcroppings of gold-carrying quartz veins. Yet, Bob occasionally picked up rocks he was sure had gold in them, and he was equally sure they hadn't fallen from the skies. Finally, in 1891, he staked out a claim in *Poverty Gulch,* a real misnomer, as it turned out.

Down in Colorado Springs a carpenter who had spent 17 summers unsuccessfully prospecting all over the Rockies, heard of Bob's claim and went around the mountain to Cripple Creek where, on July 4, 1891, he staked out *The Independence,* named in honor of the day. He was Winfield Scott Stratton, to become Cripple Creek's first gold millionaire. The news of his rich strike brought hundreds of other prospectors on the run and claims were staked by the dozens.

The Broadmoor Casino built by Pourtales, now the site of the famous Broadmoor Hotel.

Cripple Creek, looking down Bennett Street, before the fire of 1896 virtually destroyed the city.

As in other mining areas, most of these prospectors had neither money nor know-how to develop their claims. It needed capital, and that was enticed in by a German nobleman, Count James Pourtales. The Count had come to Colorado Springs some years before, and had used up his financial resources in developing a residential area at the foot of Cheyenne Mountain in the most scenic part of a dairy farm called Broadmoor in which he had acquired an interest. To supply water for his real estate development he dug a lake, the water being held back by an earthen dam. When gophers began digging holes in the dam and people feared a

flood, he concreted the dam and built a splendid *Palace of Pleasure,* the Broadmoor Casino, on top of it to prove his confidence in its safety. All this had been costly, and now the Count was broke.

When news came of the Cripple Creek strikes, the Count dashed off around the mountain to see if, by the magic of gold, he might replenish his fortune. With $2000 of his own plus $60,000 borrowed from James J. Hagerman, the Michigan-Leadville-Aspen millionaire and builder of the Colorado Midland Railroad, the Count bought the Buena Vista claim and publicly announced his purchase. This was the boost Cripple Creek needed. If the glamorous Count thought the place held promise, others felt it was worth investigating and investing in. Poor old Bob Womack sold his claim for $300,

Count James Pourtales

then saw its price go up in a few months to $50,000. It eventually produced some $5,000,000—but Bob died penniless. So it went with many of the early prospectors; only a few of them came in for the big money.

With all these people coming in to the Cripple Creek bowl, Horace Bennett and Julius Myers, owners of the *Broken Box* ranch for which Bob Womack worked, while still looking on anyone searching for gold in this unlikely spot as crazy, rushed to lay out a town—after all, people who didn't know any better might buy lots for more than the land was worth. They didn't take time to level off the main east-west street, which they named Bennett Avenue, and in one block, half of it is a dozen feet lower than the other half. It came to be a standing joke in Cripple Creek that "a man broke his neck falling off Bennett Avenue last night." The parallel street to the south was named for Mr. Myers, and here, before long, the dens of iniquity were concentrated. Sober, law-abiding, middle-aged Julius Myers never stopped shaking his head in amazement and amusement that this particular street happened to carry his name. Years later a well-known writer named Julian Street wrote a disparaging account of Myers Avenue for a national magazine and the city fathers retaliated by re-naming Myers Avenue *Julian Street.*

By the time the Cripple Creek townsite was laid out, every foot of the surrounding slopes was being picked at and staked out. A drug clerk

83

Cripple Creek's mining area, near Victor.

who couldn't see that one spot looked any more likely than the next, threw his hat in the air, dug where it fell, named his rich claim *The Pharmacist*. A blacksmith saw a pair of elk horns lying on a rock, dug, struck the Elkton. One prospector brought along some chickens so he could have an egg once in a while and put up a little pen for them. Then he decided things were moving so fast he couldn't wait for the eggs, and he began to eat the chickens. Finally only one tough old rooster was left—and a hawk swooped down and started to fly off with him. The infuriated prospector blasted the hawk to bits with his shotgun; the rooster got axed to put him out of his misery; and when the prospector cut him up, he found his craw full of high grade stones. Naturally he called the mine he dug in the little pen where the chickens had scratched the *Chicken Hawk*.

Jimmie Burns and Jimmy Doyle set their stakes around the only spot left unclaimed on Battle Mountain above Stratton's Independence, and named it the Portland, for their home town, Portland, Maine. It wasn't larger than a 50x60 foot lot, and had been claimed and abandoned half a dozen times already. They started digging—and the Portland became the richest of them all.

Battle Mountain was some six miles from Cripple Creek, and the Woods brothers, Frank and Harry, thought it about time to lay out a rival town closer to these rich mines. They named it Victor. While excavating for the Victor Hotel they struck the Gold Coin, one of the big ones. Before long two electric trolleys connected Cripple Creek and Victor, the High Line and the Low Line.

Two railroads raced each other into the bowl. First to arrive was the narrow-gauge Florence and Cripple Creek which fought its way up tortuous Phantom Canyon from Florence. Next came the Midland Terminal, connecting Cripple Creek with James J. Hagerman's Colorado Midland at Divide, 18 miles north. Several years later a group of Colorado Springs business men built the Short Line, which climbed up from Colorado Springs to Cripple Creek on the south side of the Peak. In 1901 Theodore Roosevelt was given a ride on the Short Line and expressed his feelings in words quoted countless times: "This," he said, "is scenery that bankrupts the English language." The roadbed of the Short Line is now a scenic highway, the Gold Camp Road.

Albert E. Carlton was a prime motivator in building the Midland Terminal. Bert and his brother Leslie had come to Cripple Creek at the beginning of the mining boom, grubstaked by their wealthy father. Bert was suffering from T.B. and it was hoped the pure air of the high mountain area would cure him. It did; and Albert E. Carlton went on to become the *King of Cripple Creek*. The Carltons organized a transfer company to haul freight from the Colorado Midland at Divide. Though it would mean a loss for the transfer business, Bert almost immediately began to agitate for a railroad to connect Cripple Creek with the main line of the Midland; the Midland Terminal was the result.

By the turn of the century Bert Carlton had acquired interests in many Cripple Creek businesses. About the same time the mines had reached several hundred feet in depth and were being stopped by water. There being no natural outlet to the volcanic bowl, water from melting snows seeped into the ground and into the mine shafts. Pumps were lowered down the shafts, but they were inadequate to take care of the quantity of water.

As the problem became critical Bert Carlton reminded the mine owners that he had been talking about a drainage tunnel for years. He was convinced that if the granite bowl were punctured so that the water could be drained off, millions of dollars of good ore would be uncovered. And he said he knew a man who could build such a tunnel. "Who?" The others wanted to know. "Bert Carlton," he said. Why, this must be a joke! Bert Carlton, ditch digger! Transfer man, coal dealer, railroad promoter, banker, miner, yes. But ditch digger! A vote was called for and Carlton was given a unanimous go-ahead.

By 1910 the granite rim of the golden bowl had been punctured and water was released at the rate of 8500 gallons a minute. Now mining could be carried out at lower levels. At the 1200-foot level of the Cresson the drill, surprisingly, hit a cavity. And, as though Aladdin had rubbed his magic lamp, there before the stunned miners appeared one of the wonders of the world—a giant cave encrusted with sparkling jewels. The miners waded knee deep in gold-bearing sylvanite crystals that had flaked off from the walls and ceiling of the giant vug. (Vug—a Cornish word meaning *a cavity in the rock.*) In the first four weeks they took out $1,200,000 from the Cresson Vug.

No one was more overjoyed than Mr. Carlton, though he owned no part of the Cresson—then. His satisfaction came because the vug, uncovered only because the water had been drained out of the mine, justified

Spencer Penrose

his tunnel. His next undertaking was acquisition of all the mines of Cripple Creek. He knew that bringing the mines under one management would eliminate the constant legal battles brought on by the erratic meanderings of the gold veins, as well as make for more efficient operation. By 1930 Bert Carlton owned nearly every mine in Cripple Creek. He was one of some 30 millionaires created by Cripple Creek gold.

Two others were Charles L. Tutt and Spencer Penrose. Spec Penrose had just come to Colorado Springs to visit his boyhood chum, Charlie Tutt, when the Bowl of Gold boom began. They, too, rushed to the west side of Pikes Peak and acquired the C.O.D. (Cash On Delivery) claim near Bob Womack's El Paso lode in Poverty Gulch. However, Cripple Creek gold was only the beginning of Spencer Penrose's vast fortune. The major part of it came later from copper in Utah, Arizona, and elsewhere.

Penrose, the youngest son of a prominent Philadelphia family and somewhat of a black sheep compared to his brothers, who were all

Midway point of the Manitou & Pikes Peak R.R., acquired by Penrose.

Typical freight wagon, transportation before the railroads.

successful in politics and in the professions, had fallen in love with Colorado Springs when he first came out in 1891. Now, wealthy beyond believing, he returned to that city to live and enjoy spending his money. He acquired the Cog Railway up Pikes Peak and the cable car up Mt. Manitou. He bought the carriage road up the Peak and improved and graded it for automobile traffic. (Years before, in 1900, the first auto had poked its boiling radiator up the carriage road.) He constructed a highway up Cheyenne Mountain which Robert Ripley in his "Believe It Or Not" claims is the longest road in the shortest space in the world—seven miles long, two miles straight up from bottom to top.

Penrose was a great admirer of the humorist Will Rogers, and to honor him he built the Will Rogers Shrine of the Sun at one turn on the Cheyenne Mountain road. The tower, lighted at night, is a beacon seen for miles by travelers approaching the Pikes Peak Region.

Spec always loved animals, and one of his pet projects was creation of the Cheyenne Mountain Zoo, one of the finest privately-owned zoos in the world.

All these things interested him; but building the fabulous Broadmoor Hotel was the passion of his life.

Spencer Penrose developed a basic philanthropic philosophy—that wealth should be used to benefit the region whence it came. With his lovely wife Julie, he established the El Pomar Foundation to undergird the Broadmoor financially and to aid civic, artistic, and charitable projects in Colorado Springs and throughout the state. The citizens of

Winfield Stratton

The Centennial State will be forever in debt to Spencer Penrose and his friends and associates, the Tutts—father, son, and grandsons —who have given so generously to so many projects and activities through the El Pomar Foundation.

Like Spencer Penrose the aristocrat, Winfield Scott Stratton the carpenter had become convinced, a third of a century earlier, that the wealth that came to him so unexpectedly should be used to develop the area where it originated. He never made a show of his wealth as did so many of the flamboyant mining kings. In fact, he used his mines as a bank, taking out only ore he needed for whatever project he was engaged in at the moment, leaving a balance for the future. He gave the City of Colorado Springs land on which to build a city hall and a postoffice; he built the Mining Exchange Building; he spent two million dollars modernizing the street car system; he gave generous gifts to individuals, charitable organizations, many civic activities.

Eight years after he dscovered the Independence, Stratton sold it to an English syndicate for $10,000,000. With this vast sum now to be disposed of, he set about feverishly to implement a vision he had during a critical illness. Though he was only 54, he knew time was running out for him, and he spent what little energy was left to him in perfecting his will. He was determined that his great idea would hold up in any legal proceedings that might follow the filing of his will after his death.

Winfield Scott Stratton died on September 14, 1902, and great honor was paid him. His body lay in state at the Mining Exchange Building and 9000 people filed by to look at the $3-a-day carpenter who had struck it rich and become a world figure; who had become legendary for his generosity to individuals and to his home community.

Churches, schools, charitable institutions, and individuals all were keyed up over the prospect of even more generous gifts to come. And then the will was read. After a few special bequests to relatives and friends, he directed that all the balance of his immense estate was to be used to build a home for the aged poor and for dependent children, to be called the Myron Stratton Home, in memory of his father. Little London was aghast. A gigantic poorhouse! Heaven forbid! Well, heaven didn't—but certainly a lot of human beings tried to. There were 13 years of spectacular litigation before the estate was finally settled and the Stratton Home built. Among those who tried to break the will were a dozen women, all claiming to be Stratton's widow. He had been married once, for a few months, and there was a son who Stratton said was not his. But a parade of widows!

The Myron Stratton Home, far from being a "gigantic poorhouse," became a model for other such retirement homes and is one of the things of which Colorado Springs is most proud.

* * * * *

It was an uncanny, yet fortunate, quirk of history that the influx of Cripple Creek gold into the economy came just at the time—the early 1890s—when the sky fell in on the silver-producing areas. The gold boom gave work to unemployed miners, as well as gold backing for U.S. currency. Close to a half billion dollars in gold was taken out of "The Bowl of Gold," an area only six square miles in extent.

* * * * *

An English traveler was entertained in Cripple Creek in the '90s, but found, when he started to write a thank you note to his hosts, that he'd lost the address. He was sure he remembered, however. He addressed the letter to *Lame Stream, Colorado, U.S.A.* It was delivered, the post office being clever enough to translate English into American.

Family group at Sherman, Colorado.

VII

COLORADO'S WORTHY WOMEN

" .... *the hardworking, courageous heroines*

of the mining camps and homesteads. "

very woman who crossed the plains to the mountains of Colorado in pioneer days was a heroine. It took heroic courage to leave home and parents and friends and start off for the unknown, knowing that news would be months in going in either direction, and that the chances of ever seeing loved ones again were slim.

It took heroic stamina to endure the hardships of the long journey—the jolting, rumbling trek, day after long day in covered wagons; the frightful fear—or awful actuality—of Indian raids. It took heroic fortitude to make homes out of crude shacks, to bear and rear children far from doctors or medical supplies; the many small headstones in the old cemeteries are mute evidence of the suffering and heart-break of pioneer mothers.

It took heroic strength to do the chores—rendering fat to make soap and candles; standing over washtubs with aching backs, breathing the foul steam arising from dirty linen, rubbing the skin off knuckles on the washboard; ironing with heavy sadirons heated on a wood stove.

Tears of fatigue must often have fallen onto the breadboard as these homemakers kneaded dough for bread or biscuits and managed to prepare hearty meals from scant supplies.

Of truly heroic stature were these sturdy pioneer women.

* * * * *

"I AM THE FIRST . . ."
— Julia Anna Holmes

One of the first white women to head westward across the plains in response to the cry of *Gold in Them Thar Hills!* was Julia Anna Archibald Holmes. She was certainly

Julia A. Holmes

the first to cross the plains in bloomers! She was equally certainly the first white woman to climb Pikes Peak. Julia Anna was a 20-year-old bride when she came west in 1858.

Her father had come to Kansas from his native Nova Scotia, to help the territory become a free state, and the Archibald home became one of the stations on the underground system which aided runaway slaves. Her mother was an ardent woman suffragist. So it was not surprising that, when the young bride started the long trek to the gold fields in the Rockies, she should wear the comfortable and practical "reform dress" named for Amelia Jenks Bloomer, a prominent agitator for women's rights.

When people in Lawrence, Kansas, heard of Green Russell's gold strike in the Colorado mountains, they lost no time in fitting out a party to answer the siren call of the shining metal. In the summer of 1858, a year before the Pikes Peak or Bust frenzy, they started westward in covered wagons. Julia Anna Holmes was one of two women with the group. She walked an average ten miles a day beside an ox-drawn wagon. Believing, as she did, in the right of women to equal privileges with men, she demanded that the guardmaster give her a regular turn at guarding the camp. The Captain of the Guard, however, being "conservative up to his eyes," as she wrote, refused. "He believes," she continued, "that woman is an angel—without any sense—needing the legislation of her brothers to keep her in her place; that restraint removed, she would usurp his position and then not only be no longer an angel, but unwomanly as well."

Her husband James received several flattering offers for her from the Indians, one brave offering two squaws in exchange.

By August, the group was encamped at the foot of Pikes Peak, and several men climbed the mountain. "That," said Julia Anna, "I must do." After careful preparation she and James began the climb with supplies for six days. An important item in these supplies was a copy of Emerson's Essays. On the fifth day, August 5, 1858, taking with them only their writing materials and Emerson, they made the final assault on the summit. And Julia Anna Holmes wrote, "In all probability I am the first woman who has stood upon the summit of this majestic mountain and gazed upon the wondrous scene which my eyes now behold." So far as is known, she was.

"PEACE . . . ON LONG'S PEAK" — Isabella Bird

Another woman to achieve fame in Colorado mountain-climbing history was Isabella Bird, when she climbed Long's Peak in 1873.

As a child in England, Isabella was in delicate health, and the doctor recommended a sea voyage as therapy. This would be the first of many trips to Asia, Europe, and America for Isabella. Her personal knowledge of world geography became so extensive, that in 1892 she was honored by being the first woman elected a Fellow of the Royal Geographical Society. At age 65, she was still traveling, covering 8,000 miles in 15 months on horseback in remote sections of China.

In 1873, on one of several trips to America, she spent some time in the Rocky Mountains of Colorado, and while here she climbed 14,256-foot Long's Peak. Isabella described the *Lady's Mountain Dress* she wore on the climb as well as while riding horseback many hundreds of miles, until it finally (understandably) wore out completely. "It consisted of

Isabella Bird

a half-fitting jacket, a skirt reaching to the ankles, and full Turkish trousers gathered with frills falling over the boots." In this thoroughly serviceable and feminine mountaineering costume she reached the summit of the mighty mountain. However, she was **"humiliated by her success,"** for her guide, one-eyed Mountain Jim, had to drag her up "like a bale of goods by sheer force of muscle."

After hours of terror she made the summit and "the glories of the view were burnt in upon my memory. . . . It was something, at last to stand upon the storm-rent crown of this lonely sentinel of the Rocky Range, on one of the mightiest of the vertebrae of the backbone of the North American continent, and to see the waters start for both oceans. Uplifted above love and hate and storms of passion . . . peace rested for that one bright day on Long's Peak."

Isabella described every activity and strange sight encountered on her many travels in letters to her sister, and each set was later published in book form, among them her experiences in the Rockies. Her description of Denver gives a vivid vignette of life in Colorado Territory just before statehood. She saw few women, but there were "men in every kind of rig . . . hunters and trappers in buckskins . . . men of the plains with belts and revolvers, in great blue cloaks, relics of the war; teamsters in fringed leather suits; horsemen in fur coats and caps and buffalo-hide boots; Broadway dandies in yellow kid gloves; and rich English sporting tourists, supercilious-looking." Adding to the harlequin appearance of Denver streets, she noted, were the many colorfully-dressed Indians.

"AMERICA THE BEAUTIFUL"
— Katherine Lee Bates.

As time wore on, it became easier to reach the top of one mountain, at least— Pikes Peak. By 1891 a carriage road wound upward and a cog railway inched its way to the top. Jolting up in a carriage in 1893 was a visiting professor at the Colorado College summer school in Colorado Springs. Katherine Lee Bates taught English at Wellesley for 40 years, but her national

Katherine Lee Bates

93

and enduring fame rests on this jaunt to the summit of Pikes Peak in the summer of 1893. Miss Bates was overwhelmed by the majestic view and cried, as have countless others, "Oh, Beautiful!" She lifted her head and added, "Such spacious skies!" She looked across the limitless plains to the east and remembered the wind-waved gold of vast wheat fields she had passed through on her way to Colorado. The purple mountain shadows crept upward.

The great significance of her beloved land flowed through her whole being, and suddenly, there on the summit of Pikes Peak, the inspiration for the poem *America The Beautiful* sprang into the mind of Katherine Lee Bates:

> "O beautiful for spacious skies,
> For amber waves of grain;
> For purple mountain majesties
> Above the fruited plain —
>
> America! America! God shed His grace on thee,
> And crown thy good with brotherhood,
> From sea to shining sea."

"RAMONA" — Helen Hunt Jackson

These three women touched Colorado only transiently; those we meet next called Colorado *home*.

The most famous woman to live in Colorado was unquestionably the author of *Ramona*, Helen Hunt Jackson. As a little girl in Amherst, Massachusetts, where she was born in 1830, she had the literary stimulus of a father who was a professor of Languages and Philosophy. However, Helen grew up a gay, lively, attractive young woman with no literary thoughts of her own, and when she was 21 she married an army officer, Edward Hunt. They had two sons, one of whom lived less than a year. In 1863, during the Civil War, Major Hunt was accidently killed while testing a primitive submarine of his own invention. Two years later, nine-year-old Rennie died of diphtheria. The heartbroken mother wrote her first poem, *Lifted Over*. Published in 1865, just at the close of the Civil War, its words comforted many another grieving mother:

Helen Hunt Jackson

> ". . . So did our Father watch the precious boy . . .
> He saw the sweet limbs faltering . . .
> So reached from heaven, and lifting the dear child
> . . . He put him down beyond all hurt . . . and bade
> Him wait for me. Shall I not then be glad,
> And, thanking God, press on to overtake?"

After the war the 35-year-old widow began seriously to write. Poems, articles, childrens' stories flowed from her pen and were published regularly in such erudite magazines as the Atlantic Monthly, the Nation, and others. Since, in the 1860s, writing for publication was considered by many to be "unwomanly," the budding author identified herself only as *H.H.* Her writing brought her enough income to make possible a year traveling in Europe. Soon after her return home her first book of poems, *Verses, by H.H.*, and her first book of prose, *Bits of Travel*, were published. She turned to fiction, and, still refusing to own up to her authorship, she chose the pseudonym *Saxe Holm*. The stories were popular, and there was much speculation as to just who Saxe Holm was. It was years before it came out that *he* was actually Helen Hunt, or *H.H.* She was recognized as America's most prolific woman writer, and Ralph Waldo Emerson called her the greatest American woman poet.

H.H. did some book reviewing, one of the books being Anna Leonowen's *An English Governess in the Siamese Court,* and Helen had the thrill of meeting Anna. How unbelieving both would have been could they have known that a hundred years later Anna's story would be transformed into one of the most popular musicals of all time, *The King and I.*

H.H. was definitely not in sympathy with the Suffragettes, and wrote a story, *Wanted—A Home,* in which she protested, as she said, "the wrong side of the womans rights movement."

She became ill; and with "galloping consumption" always a possibility —her mother had been a T.B. victim—she came West, to Colorado Springs, to benefit from the dry air and the bright sunshine. Here she met a bachelor, William S. Jackson, five years younger than she. He was immediately attracted to the vibrant, exciting, famous widow, and set out to persuade her to marry him. He had come west to be Secretary-Treasurer of General Palmer's D&RG railroad, and was one of the founders of Colorado Springs. Two years later Helen Hunt became Mrs. William S. Jackson. They moved into a fine home built by the carpenter Winfield Scott Stratton, later to become the first Cripple Creek gold millionaire.

Marriage did not curb the author's impulse to write, and a succession of poems, articles, and books were sent to publishers back east during these early years in Colorado Springs.

Though she loved the mountains, Mrs. Jackson missed her literary friends and the stimulating intellectual life she had known in the East, and she made frequent trips back to New England. On one of these she heard an emotional account by a Ponca Indian chieftain named Standing Bear, of the sufferings of the Indians who had been dispossessed of their lands. She was so incensed that she set out on a humanitarian crusade to restore basic human rights to America's natives.

She spent months in the Bureau of Indian Affairs making a detailed study of treaties made with the Indians and broken almost before the ink on the signatures was dry. The result was a carefully documented "sketch," as she called it, of the government's dealings with some of the Indian tribes, titled *A Century of Dishonor.* In the Author's Note at the beginning, she says her object was "to show our causes for national shame in the matter of our treatment of the Indians" from the founding of the country in 1776 to the 1880s.

A Century of Dishonor was published in 1881. At her own expense, Mrs. Jackson sent a copy to each congressman. She was reviled, as are all reformers, by some; yet the book had impact—no one could ignore her massive indictment of official policies regarding the Indians. President Chester Arthur appointed her a Commissioner of Indian Affairs, and she was sent to observe the situation of the Indians of southern California. Here she was inspired to write the novel, *Ramona*. Se had "tried to attack the peoples conscience directly in a *Century of Dishonor;*" now she "sugared the pill," presenting the Indians' plight in story form. *Ramona* was ranked with Harriet Beecher Stowe's *Uncle Tom's Cabin* as one of the two great ethical novels of the century.

Interestingly enough, with the modern emphasis on minority groups, *A Century of Dishonor* was reprinted in 1965 and is used as a college textbook. *Ramona* has gone through over 300 printings, and has been made into play, moving picture, and pageant.

Mrs. Jackson died in August, 1885, when she was only 54. Two years later the Dawes Act was enacted. This law allotted land directly to the Indians, provided for their citizenship, and abandoned the unwieldy concept that each tribe was an independent nation to be dealt with by treaty. Helen Hunt Jackson's impassioned plea for the nation to correct its history of Indian mistreatment had begun to bear fruit.

SCIENTIST-HUMANITARIAN — Dr. Florence Rena Sabin

The work of another Colorado woman gained international recognition in the field of science.

Central City was still a rough mining camp in 1871 when Florence Sabin was born. As a child she showed intense interest and remarkable skills in scientific subjects. She went east for medical studies; with her degree gained she became the first woman professor at Johns Hopkins University. Every medical student at Johns Hopkins from 1902 to 1925 had Anatomy as a required subject in the Freshman year, and was exposed to Dr. Sabin's inspirational teaching.

Dr. Florence Rena Sabin

She gained fame as a medical researcher and humanitarian, as well as teacher. International recognition came for her cellular studies at the Rockefeller Institute in New York, and for her fight to improve health laws and standards in her home state of Colorado. This last humanitarian work came after Dr. Sabin, now in her 70s, had retired and returned to Denver. She led the people of her native state in a movement for better health, and shepherded through the State

Legislature the *Sabin Health Bills* which resulted in one of the best health programs in the United States.

Many honors came to Dr. Sabin. She was the first woman to be elected to life membership in the National Academy of Sciences. She was given 15 honorary degrees. In the 1930s she was called *The greatest living woman scientist and one of the great scientists of all time.*

To cap the climax of her enduring fame, a heroic bronze statue of her was placed in Statuary Hall in the National Capitol in Washington.

From mining camp babe to this epitome of recognition—that was the life story of one of Colorado's worthy women, Dr. Florence Sabin.

"FOR ALL WHO WISH TO LEARN" — Emily Griffith

In the early years of this century few people thought about adult education. Emily Griffith was one who did. A phrase had burned itself into her consciousness as a child and it led to a dream that culminated in the *Emily Griffith Opportunity School* in Denver, one of the first efforts at providing education for all ages.

Near her childhood home in Cincinnati the Erie Canal boats tied up at the dock at night. On one hung a sign, lighted by a lantern: "FOR ALL WHO WISH TO LEARN." People could come aboard for a night's schooling. It was this phrase that fired the little girl's imagination; these were the words that appeared, years later, below the name *Emily Griffith Opportunity School* on a building in Denver.

From the start, Emily knew she wanted to be a teacher; and when, at age 14, now living in Nebraska, she was faced with having to become a

Emily Griffith

breadwinner, she applied for a job and was interviewed by members of the school board. One thought she was too young; another said, "She's too pretty"; a third noted, "But she's smart." She got the job and began her teaching career. Since many of her pupils were older than she and in higher grades she studied by lamplight to keep ahead of the class.

The family moved to Colorado and Emily continued her teaching in a section of Denver where there were many foreigners and disadvantaged families. The conviction grew in her that something must be done to provide education for these people. In 1910 someone asked her, "Emily, what is your greatest desire?" She thought for a moment, then put into words the dream that had been with her from childhood, for education "for all who wish to learn." Summarizing, she said, "It would be an opportunity school"—and so the name was born.

Emily was in her late 30s when, on September 7, 1916, she went with many misgivings to open the doors of the *Emily Griffith Opportunity*

97

Class in session at Emily Griffith Opportunity School, Denver.

Scene from the 1880's at Mineral Point, Colorado.

School. Suppose no one came? Suppose some did come, but only to scoff? A little old man hobbled up and said, "I thought I might learn to make signs." "What kind of signs?" "Oh, signs I could sell—signs people need. Like 'Fresh Vegetables'; 'Look Out for the Dog'; 'Yard Eggs'." Emily promised to teach him. About that time a streetcar came by and disgorged most of its passengers, all of whom came to the door, and Emily and her staff were swamped with pupils and requests. One young girl wanted "to learn how to make pretty things—I jest loves pretty things, soft things like velvet." They taught her to make flowers and hats. A man wanted "the chance to finish the 8th grade so I can take the barber's exam." Another wanted " 'nuff figerin' to plaster." And so it went.

At the end of a week 1400 people had come to the school. A hundred had signed up to learn typing—on the one typewriter. For 13 hours, five days a week, pupils appeared in relays. There were 2400 pupils the first year.

Soon after the opening a boy fainted in class, and Emily realized that many of her pupils were hungry. She and her sister Florence started a soup kitchen. Their mother made the soup at home, the sisters carried the full kettle of soup to the school on the streetcar, served it, and cleaned up afterward. As many as 200 bowls of soup were served each evening.

Emily told her faculty, which soon numbered 38, "By their joy ye shall know them—give a pupil an assignment he can do so he will have a sense of joy and accomplishment." "A boy," she said, "may never have been anybody anywhere else, but he is somebody here." One evening a young tramp came to the door and muttered, "Well, tell me to move on—that's what the cop told me." Answered Emily, "We don't do that, son—we tell folks to move *in*."

One man brought his wife to school to learn to read; and it delighted Emily to watch them walking down the street proudly spelling out words on the signs. A man of 70 received his high school diploma. The students ranged in age from 16 to 75. Miss Griffith summed it up: "When a boy comes to school with his father and they both learn 'What is so rare as a day in June' and then they say it together as they drive up and down alleys cleaning out ashpits, that's what Opportunity School means."

In June, 1947, headlines screamed "EMILY GRIFFITH AND HER SISTER SLAIN IN CABIN HOME!" Each had been shot in the head. Emily Griffith had no enemy in the world; no motive could be found for her violent death; the murderer was never caught.*

The life of Emily Griffith, whose one idea was to help people who needed help, was brutally snuffed out; but that idea still thrives, and the Emily Griffith Opportunity School is looked upon by people all over the world as a model of what an adult educational system should be.

---

*Authorities concluded that it was a mercy killing by a close friend. It was never proved.

***Portions of *Dr. Florence Sabin: Colorado Woman of the Century* (1959) and *Emily Griffith and the Opportunity School* (1954) reprinted by special permission of the Author and Publisher, Elinor Bluemel.

CLARA BROWN — Adventurer at Heart

These six vignettes have presented women educated far beyond the average pioneer home-maker—those hard-working, courageous heroines of the mining camps and the bleak homesteads. The woman whose story closes this selection of Colorado's colorful characters is chosen because her life, so vastly different from that of any of her sisters, is yet one of the most inspiring and heart-warming. It is a story in which a life well lived receives its just reward; a story where everything comes out right in the end.

Clara Brown

Clara Brown was black. She was a freed slave, given her freedom by her owners in Kentucky, who recognized her unusual qualities, in 1859, several years before the Civil War. Years before, she had married another slave; later, they and their daughter Liza Jane had been sold on the auction block to different owners. Clara knew that her husband had died; her search for Liza Jane became the passion of her life.

Her former owners gave her money to get to Leavenworth, Kansas, where wagon trains for the Rockies were formed. Even she, a slave, had heard vague rumors of the trek to the *mountains beyond sundown*. Clara, in her late 50s, was an adventurer at heart, and she joined the other pioneers. There were those who raised a cry of dissent when a Black appeared on the scene. But Clara contracted to cook for the wagoneers, and they started off for Colorado.

Clara was an ardent Baptist and she had a warm love for everyone, black or white. When one man on the wagon train became ill, it was Clara who helped his wife nurse him and bring him through. When they reached Auraria, across Cherry Creek from the embryo town of Denver, Clara and this couple stopped at the City Bakery where, the sign said, hot meals were served.

The talkative German proprietor proudly told them that a Methodist mission was soon to be set up. Religion, of whatever brand, being so close to Clara's heart, she was as excited as he. Then, to her amazement, Herr Reitze asked if she could help him in the Bakery. Clara could hardly believe her ears. Never, she exclaimed, had she dreamed of such help from a stranger. Answered the German, "I am not a stranger, Sister Brown. Aren't we brothers and sisters in Christ?"

Like the other pioneers, Clara's main objective was to get to the mountains. She met a prospector who told her that the men in the mining camps detested washing their own garments above all chores. Now washing and ironing were Clara's greatest talents. If she could only get to Central City and start a laundry! But she knew that no Black could buy a stagecoach ticket in Colorado any more than in Kentucky.

She asked the prospector if he would take her and her tubs and boiler to Central City, pretending she was his hired help, but actually accepting full fare from her. He agreed—and Clara's future was decided. She rented a run-down cabin and started her laundry. By the end of the Civil War, Clara, ever thrifty, had a nice nest egg, including property and mining claims. And now it was safe for her to go back to Kentucky. Her idea was to find not only Liza Jane, but all her relatives, and take them back with her to Colorado!

Her former owners were as happy to see her as they were amazed. They sorrowfully reminded her that her relatives would all be too old for such a journey, even if she could find them. And she searched for Liza Jane in vain. Then it seemed a voice came to her, reminding her that all men were her brothers, whether they were blood kin or not. It was in her power to help folks unable to help themselves. She had enough money to pay the fare of 16 Blacks from Kentucky to Colorado, and she felt certain she could find work for them once they got there. So she and her bewildered proteges started off to Leavenworth to begin the long crossing of the plains.

She was genuinely surprised at the cordial welcome she received in Central City. To do what she had done would have been an achievement by anybody at any time. But to carry out such an involved project at that time, and at her age—she was now in her late 60s—using money she had earned by sheer hard work and shrewd investment—such a story stirred people's imagination.

Clara had kept as accurate an account of the expenditures for her expedition as her limited knowledge of arithmetic allowed. It seemed like an awful lot, and she asked a lawyer friend about it. He went over all the receipts—and gave her the terrible news that she had been robbed of nearly $4000 in Leavenworth. How many backbreaking hours she had spent over a washtub to accumulate that!

In 1879, now 79, Clara heard about great numbers of Blacks pouring out of the south into Kansas and being in dire straits. Maybe Liza Jane was among them! Back Clara went, ministering to the frightened, lonely, destitute people in her usual loving way. But no one knew anything of Liza Jane.

Now, for the first time in her life, Clara became ill. She needed to be at a lower altitude, and a kindly man in Denver offered her a little house in which she could spend the rest of her life. For now her resources were exhausted, and she could no longer earn her own living.

At Christmas, 1881, Clara received a formal document. As an 1859-er and an outstanding citizen of both Denver and Central City, she was hereby certified as a member of the Society of Colorado Pioneers, an exclusive group that, heretofore, had accepted neither women nor blacks. Think of it! This honor paid to a former slave, a washerwoman, now an impoverished old woman nearly helpless from a physical disability!

By 1882 Clara had resigned herself to the fact that she would never see Liza Jane this side of heaven. After all, it had been more than 50 years since their separation. And then, the miracle. A friend in Council Bluffs, Iowa, wrote that she was sure someone she had met must be Liza

Jane—a laundress, in her late 50s, with a daughter Cindy, a cleaning-woman. As ill as she was, Clara borrowed money to go back to see if, at long last, she had found her Liza Jane. She had.

The story got out, and a reporter sensed a first-rate human interest feature. It touched the hearts of people in churches, clubs, businesses, citizens generally. And money flowed in—enough, even, to allow Cindy to accompany her grandmother back to Denver. Cindy stayed, and soon built up her own modest business, cleaning and washing.

In the summer of 1885 Cindy had to write her mother the distressing news that Clara was failing fast, and Liza Jane came to Denver as quickly as she could.

In September, Cindy and Liza Jane dressed Aunt Clara, her body now swollen with edema, in a new calico dress, white apron, and colorful turban; and two men carried her to a buggy—to go to the annual banquet of the Society of Colorado Pioneers.

At the hall she was propped up in a chair, and Liza Jane unobtrusively fed her. The speaker, a former mayor of Denver, eulogized her, dwelling especially on her long quest for Liza Jane as an almost unequalled example of love, loyalty, and faith.

It was a great evening for Clara Brown. The next month she died, age 85, honored by all who had ever known her.

***Portions of *'Aunt' Clara Brown, Story of a Black Pioneer* reprinted by permission of the Author, Kathleen Bruyn, and the Publisher, Pruett Publishing Company, Boulder, Colorado. (1970).

All dressed up for a tour of Denver, 1906.

Typical general store in Colorado at the end of the century.

Smuggler-Union Mill at Telluride, about 1912.

VIII.

WHAT'S IN A NAME

" names .... conjure up all sorts of stories .... "

olorado's colorful characters are matched by her colorful
names. The Indians, the Spanish, the French, all left their
mark indelibly on the map and the culture of Colorado. There
are Indian words like Uncompahgre, meaning red lake, from the reddish
hot springs of Ouray, where the Uncompahgre River begins; Curecanti,
the name of the chief who directed the Ute Bear Dance festival each
spring; Shavano, blue flower; Saguache, blue earth; Tomichi, hot water;
Apishapa, stinking water; Muckawango, place where bears walk.

Names of the Indian chiefs themselves are picturesque, to say the least:
Roman Nose, Black Kettle, Tall Bull, Dull Knife, Wild Hog, Little Wolf,
Left Hand.

The Spanish gave the name Colorado, meaning red, first to the muddy
Colorado River; then the name attached itself to the territory, and at
statehood in 1876, to the state. They named one magnificent mountain
range Sangre de Cristo—Blood of Christ—from the red glow on the crest
as the sun rises in the east. Buena Vista means good view, rather an
understatement. Other interesting Spanish names: Culebra (snake);
Hermoso (beautiful); Huerfano (orphan); Tejon (badger).

The Spanish also gave a river the mouth-filling name of El Rio de las
Animas Perdidos en Purgatorio (River of the Lost Souls in Purgatory).
The story goes that a quarrel arose between two leaders of a Spanish
expedition, and one killed the other. The priest accompanying the expedition refused to continue with a murderer, and turned back with a
handful of followers. The others went on, and nothing more was heard
of them until a later expedition came upon rusted armor and skeletons
pierced by arrows along the banks of a stream, obviously the scene of
an Indian massacre. As no priest had been with the party, the men died
without receiving the last rites of the church, and their souls, therefore,
were presumably wandering forever in purgatory—hence the name. Later,
the French used their word, *Purgatoire*. Later still, to cowboys herding
cattle on the plains, the word sounded like *Picketwire*. To further confuse

104

the issue, the name of the river appears on maps variously as Las Animas, Purgatory, Purgatoire, or Picketwire.

In addition to putting their stamp on the Purgatoire River, the French left us another name by which to recall their passage through Colorado: Cache la Poudre River. A group of hunters hid, or "cached" their gunpowder along the stream banks.

* * * * *

The mining era added picturesque words to our vocabulary: paydirt, bedrock, mother lode, high grading, for example. High grading was any method the miners could think of for taking ore out of the mines for themselves. Some took off their hats while they worked—and at night washed the gold dust out of their hair. One man really had it made. He plastered his unruly hair down with grease, and several times the normal amount of dust stuck to it. Others made false brims for their helmets, or false soles or heels for their shoes, or hidden pockets in their clothes. Millions of dollars worth of ore were carted off, and the mine owners never did find a totally efficient way to stop the thievery.

The names chosen for mines conjure up all sorts of stories. Many are named for women, few for men—which says a lot about the loneliness of a prospector's life. It doesn't take much imagination to picture what was in the prospectors' minds when they gave these names to their claims:

Aftermath	Hard Money	Rattler
Busted Nugget	Last Chance	Revenge
Careless Boy	Little Fraud	Smuggler
Compromise	Little Tycoon	Silent Friend
Country Boy	Lost Trail	Sleeping Pet
Flat Broke	Miser's Dream	Slip Up
Golden Rule	Neglected	Snowstorm
Ground Hog	No-Name	What Is It?

That "hope springs eternal" in the miner's breast, is evidenced in such names as these:

Coming Wonder	Hunkidori	Revenue
Cracker Jack	Lucky Strike	Royal Flush
Golden Fleece	Nest Egg	Smile of Fortune
Hidden Treasure	Payrock	U.S. Bank

But is there meaning in these names?

Butterfly-Terrible	Lackawanna (later	Pie Plant (was this
Blistered Horn	dubbed *Lackamoney*	a rhubarb?—Ed.)
The Bloated Notary	Lion's Roost (Bird or	Resurrection
Inter-Ocean	Beast?—Ed.)	Spring Chicken
Kreutzer Sonata	Old Hundred (the	
	Doxology?—Ed.)	

A story is told of the Bobtail Mine in Central City. It seems a sedate spinster could not bring herself to say such a word, and called the mine, instead, *the Robert Appendage.*

105

EPILOGUE

In 1873 Ferdinand V. Hayden made a survey of Colorado Territory and reported his findings in a monumental *Geological and Geographical Atlas of Colorado.* The final paragraph is worth recalling. After describing the Tertiary geologic age of the giant mammals as having *life and beauty everywhere—and man, the great destroyer, had not yet come,* he concludes, ". . . Cities will grow colossal in size, then gray with age, then fall into decadence and their sites be long forgotten . . . near the city sites sediments will be full of relics that will illustrate and explain the mingled comedy and tragedy of human life. These relics the geologist of the future will gather and study and moralize over, as we do the record of the Tertiary ages. Let us hope that this future man, purer in morals and clearer in intellect than we, may find as much to admire in the records of this first epoch of the Reign of Man, as we do in those of the reign of mammals."

May *man, the great destroyer,* learn before it is too late to become *man, the preserver* of this wonderful land—Colorado the Magnificent, America the Beautiful.

CHRONOLOGY

(Dates starred are expanded in the text.)

Some 10,000 to 30,000 years ago—Colorado's earliest-known inhabitants, Stone Age savages, roam the plains, then vanish.

c. 100 B.C.-100 A.D.—People skilled in weaving baskets come into the mesas in southwestern Colorado, then disappear.

c. 400-800 A.D.—Another group, characterized by heads flattened by the use of hard cradle boards, builds cliff dwellings at Mesa Verde and elsewhere in the southwest. About 1300 they pass from the scene, leaving no trace except their astonishing dwellings.

1540—When the Spaniards conquered Mexico, the native Indians told them fabulous tales of the riches of *The Seven Cities of Cibola* and *Quivira.* In 1540 Francisco Coronado, with a splendid cavalcade, started northward to search for them. They marched as far as the Kansas plains, but the only "cities" they found were Indian pueblos. Disillusioned and weary, Coronado and his bedraggled army turned back toward Mexico. His expedition is pertinent to Colorado history because now for the first time the Indians saw horses. By raiding subsequent expeditions, and by breeding, the Plains Indians built up large strings of swift ponies and became expert horsemen, giving them a mobility that was devastating to the pioneers who were to come in the mid-1800s.

1682—Sieur de la Salle, French explorer, floating the length of the Mississippi, claims all lands drained by the Father of Waters (including, of course, those that have their source in the Colorado mountains) for France. By 1700 French influence was strong among the Indians of the eastern plains, and French traders were pushing ever south-westward into Spanish territory.

1706—Juan de Uribarri (sometimes spelled Ulibarri), pursuing runaway Indian slaves toward the Arkansas Valley, becomes alarmed at evidence of French penetration, and takes formal possession of the eastern plains of Colorado in the name of King Philip V of Spain.

1739—The Mallet brothers, Peter and Paul, lead the most important of several French expeditions that entered Colorado. Leaving the Missouri, they follow a river they name the Platte, meaning *flat.* They soon turn south and cross Kansas to the Arkansas, which they follow into Colorado, eventually arriving at Santa Fe.

Even into the mid-1700s, French map-makers in Paris knew little about the country west of the Mississippi and the Missouri except tales told adventurous Frenchmen by the Indians. The map-makers construed exaggerated tales of rivers and lakes as being a continuous water passage to the western ocean, a highway of floating commerce to the Orient. A map of 1752 showed

107

a *Sea of the Orient* which submerged a large part of northern Colorado. It was believed by many that the Mallets were on Chinese soil when they were tramping across Colorado.

1761—Juan Maria Rivera searches for gold in Colorado mountains; others follow.

1763—France cedes territory west of the Mississippi to Spain.

1800—Spain cedes Louisiana Territory back to France.

*1803—United States acquires part of Colorado through Louisiana Purchase.

*1806—Lt. Zebulon Pike sent to discover source of Red River, southwestern boundary of Louisiana Purchase, but he never reaches it.

1819—U.S. and Spain agree to fix boundary at Arkansas River, thence northward along Continental Divide.

*1820—Major Stephen Long sent to explore country between the Mississippi and the Rocky Mountains. Dr. Edwin James, naturalist and historian of expedition, leads first recorded ascent of Pikes Peak.

*1820-1840—Era of Mountain Men—the trappers and traders.

*1822—General William Ashley forms Rocky Mountain Fur Company.

*1828-1832—William and Charles Bent and Ceran St. Vrain build Bent's Fort near present site of La Junta.

1836—Texas becomes independent republic and claims narrow strip of mountain territory in Colorado.

1842-1853—Lt. John C. Fremont undertakes five exploration trips into Rocky Mountains, hiring Kit Carson, Jim Bridger, and other Mountain Men as guides.

1846—Col. Stephen W. Kearney (or Kearny) leads Army of the West through southeastern Colorado during Mexican War en route to conquest of New Mexico, which he accomplishes without firing a shot.

1848—Mexico cedes to U.S. areas in what became Colorado that were not included in Louisiana Purchase.

1850—Federal government purchases Texas' claims in Colorado. U.S. now has title to entire area.

1852—First permanent white settlements in Colorado founded in San Luis Valley by immigrants from New Mexico.

1853—Capt. John W. Gunnison leads exploring party across mountains seeking feasible railroad route; explores Black Canyon of the Gunnison. . . . October, he and all but four of his expedition are killed in an Indian raid in Utah.

1854—Ute Indians massacre inhabitants of Fort Pueblo on Christmas Day.

*1858—Green Russell, miner from Georgia gold fields, and party raise color on Cherry Creek, precipitating gold rush of the next year. Auraria (meaning gold) and Denver (named for governor of Kansas Territory which then included Colorado) founded on present site of Denver.

*1859—March 9, first stagecoach with mail for Cherry Creek settlements sets out from Leavenworth, Kansas. . . . Apr. 23, William N.

108

Byers issues first copy of Rocky Mountain News, first newspaper in Colorado, published continuously since . . . May 6, *Red-Bearded* John Gregory makes famous strike in Gregory Gulch, and Black Hawk and Central City boom. The gulch connecting the two soon is called *The richest square mile on earth.* . . . George Jackson makes rich strike at Idaho Springs. . . . Horace Greeley, editor of N.Y. Tribune, arrives by stagecoach and writes glowing account of the gold that he *washed with my own hands and saw with my own eyes.* . . . June 11, Rocky Mountain News issues first *extry*, printed on brown wrapping paper, to headline Greeley's report. . . . George Griffith makes strike at Georgetown. . . . Summer: Pikes Peak or Bust gold rush brings thousands across plains in covered wagons. . . . Oct. 3, O. J. Goldrick opens first school in Denver with 13 pupils. . . . Committee appointed to organize *Jefferson Territory* to govern gold camps.

1860—Abe Lee looks in pan he's just dipped into stream near present Leadville and sees so much color that he cries out "Lord A'Mighty! I've got all Californy in my pan!"—and the rush was on to California Gulch (later, Leadville). . . . In Denver, banks charged interest of 10 to 25 percent a month; Baltimore oysters were offered at $16 a gallon; gold dust was principal medium of exchange—a pinch between thumb and forefinger represented 25¢.

*1861—Congress establishes Colorado Territory with boundaries of present state. Name chosen because Colorado River (named by Spaniards for its red, muddy color) rises in the state. . . . President Lincoln appoints William Gilpin first Territorial governor. [Later, a county was named for Gilpin. No one could have foreseen that untold millions would be taken out of the hills and canyons that made up "The Kingdom of Gilpin"—the Central City area.] . . . September, first Assembly meets, creates 17 counties, authorizes University, selects Colorado City at foot of Pikes Peak as Territorial capital, appoints Henry M. Teller and Jerome B. Chaffee as state's first senators. [Teller was a mining, railroad, and hotel man—his family operated far-famed Teller House in Central City for 63 years; he served in Congress 29 years and was Secretary of the Interior in President Arthur's cabinet. Chaffee organized the First National Bank of Denver.] . . . Census shows population of Territory to be 25,371.

*1862—Second Territorial Legislature meets at Colorado City, adjourns to Denver, and selects Golden as new capital. . . . First tax-supported schools established. . . . First oil well drilled near Florence. . . . President Lincoln appoints John Evans to succeed Gilpin as Territorial Governor.

*1863—Telegraph line links Denver with east. Ten words to New York cost $9.10. . . . Plains Indians raid wagon trains and outlying ranches. Citizens demand revenge, which culminates in Sand Creek Massacre.

*1864—Massacre of Indians at Sand Creek on November 29, 1864, stirs Cheyennes and Arapahos to fresh violence and overland trails are often closed. In Denver supplies dwindle and prices soar.

1867—Denver selected as permanent Territorial capital. At close of Civil War, troops are sent to Colorado plains and gradually overcome hostile Indians.

*1868—Nathaniel P. Hill inaugurates era of hard-rock mining by erecting new type smelter at Black Hawk.

*1870—Population: 39,864. . . . David H. Moffat builds Denver-Pacific Railroad to connect Denver with Union Pacific at Cheyenne, Wyo. . . . Horace Greeley sends Nathan C. Meeker with 50 families to establish Union Colony, calling it *Greeley*. [The colonists were expected to live by strict rules, one of them being "Thou shalt not sell liquid damnation within the lines of the colony." The colonists brought the valley of the Cache la Poudre and South Platte to bountiful production by irrigation. First sizable industry was tanning of buffalo hides.]

*1871—General William J. Palmer builds Denver & Rio Grande Railroad south from Denver and founds Colorado Springs.

1872—W.A.H. Loveland constructs Colorado Central Railroad to connect Denver with Black Hawk.

*1873—Gold and silver discoveries in San Juan Mountains attract prospectors and miners to southwest Colorado. . . . Ute Indians are dispossessed of western slope territory held by treaty with federal government.

1874—Territorial Legislature appropriates $15,000 for University of Colorado at Boulder on condition equal sum be raised by that city. . . . School of Mines opens at Golden.

1876—Aug. 1—Colorado admitted to Union as 38th state. Called *The Centennial State* because nation was celebrating its own Centennial in 1876. John L. Routt, last appointed Territorial governor, becomes state's first elected governor. [Colorado is 8th largest state and has 75% of all area in U.S. over 10,000 feet. More than 1000 peaks are at least two miles high; of these, 53 rise to over 14,000 feet above sea level. State flower: blue columbine; state bird: Lark Bunting; state tree: Colorado blue spruce.]

*1877—Heavy black sand and boulders that annoyed miners at California Gulch is found to be rich carbonate of lead, carrying silver, and the silver boom is on in Leadville. . . . University of Colorado opens at Boulder with two teachers and 44 students.

*1878-79—"Royal Gorge Railroad War" between General Palmer's D&RG and the Santa Fe.

1878—Leadville is incorporated; is country's highest city . . . . Central City Opera House (present building) opens . . . First telephones installed in Denver.

*1879—Nathan C. Meeker, founder of Greeley, becomes Indian Agent on White River. He and several employees are slain in Ute uprising.

1880—Population: 194,327.

110

*1881—Ute tribes removed from western Colorado to Utah reservation . . . . Sept. 5, Tabor Opera House in Denver opens . . . Colorado **Fuel & Iron Company founded; sold in 1903 to Rockefeller interests.**

1883—First electric lights installed in Denver.

1886—Denver Union Stockyards established.

1888—Band of Utes under Colorow make last Indian raid into Colorado; they are defeated and returned to Utah reservation.

*1890—Population: 413,249 . . . . Passage of Sherman Silver Purchase Act raises price of silver to more than $1.00 an ounce. New rich silver strikes are made in San Juans . . . . July 4, 20-ton cornerstone of State Capitol is laid; contains Bible, flags and Constitution of U.S. and Colorado, state historical data, walking stick made from a piece of Old Ironsides.

*1891—Robert Womack finds gold in Cripple Creek. . . . Pikes Peak Cog Railroad begins operation.

*1893—Repeal of Sherman Silver Purchase Act strikes silver mining a paralyzing blow. . . . Nov. 2, Colorado is second state to extend suffrage to women.

*1894—State Capitol completed at cost of $2,500,000.

1899—First beet sugar refinery built at Grand Junction.

*1900—Population: 539-700. . . . Cripple Creek becomes second richest gold camp in world (first is in South Africa).

*1903-04—Mine, mill, and smelter workers strike in many places for higher wages and better working conditions. At Cripple Creek strike results in much property destruction and loss of life and public indignation is so strong that Union is expelled for good. . . . Uncompahgre irrigation project, first of federal government reclamation projects in Colorado, is authorized.

1904—U.S. Mint in Denver issues first coins. . . . June 29, Mesa Verde National Park is created by Congress.

1908—July 7, Denver Municipal Auditorium seating 12,500, is completed in time for Democratic National Convention. . . . Colorado Museum of Natural History is opened. . . . Capitol building, in use since 1896, completed and dedicated. Cost, nearly $3,000,-000; would take at least $15,000,000 to duplicate today.

1910—Population: 799,024. . . . First airplane flight in Denver.

1914—Strike of coal miners is climaxed by *Battle of Ludlow* near Trinidad in which several women and children die during hostilities between miners and militia.

1915—January 12, Rocky Mountain National Park is created by Congress.

*1916—Emily Griffith Opportunity School is opened in Denver.

1918—More than 125,000 Colorado citizens register for W.W. I draft.

1920—Population: 939,629.

1921—Pueblo suffers disastrous flood with an estimated 100 people drowned and property losses over $20,000,000.

1922—First commercial radio license issued in Colorado.

*1927—Moffat Railroad Tunnel under Continental Divide, between East Portal and Winter Park, completed at cost of $18,000,000.
1930—Population: 1,035,791.
1932-37—Prolonged drought and high winds cause tremendous damage through soil erosion in southeastern Colorado.
*1932—Central City Opera House restored. . . . July, first annual theatrical festival opens in Central City with Lillian Gish in *Camille*.
1934—More than $3,000,000,000 in gold bullion is stored in Denver mint.
1935—With Dotsero Cut-off completed, Denver, for first time, is on direct transcontinental railroad route, through Moffat tunnel.
1937—U.S. Army Air Corps establishes Lowry Field near Denver.
1940—Population: 1,123,296.
1941—Camp Carson established south of Colorado Springs; becomes permanent Fort on Aug. 16, 1954.
Colorado's history does not end here; but during World War II and in the Nuclear Age that followed, events moved too fast to be noted in this Chronology.
1950—Population: 1,325,089.
1960—Population: 1,753,947.
1970—Population: 2,207,259

ILLUSTRATION CREDITS

Permission to use the photographs and sketches on the listed pages is gratefully acknowledged.

Colorado State Historical Society: 36, 37, 39, 40, 44, 55, 58, 67, 68, 69, 70, 88, 96, 98, 100.

Denver Public Library, Western History Collection: Pike Frontispiece, 2, 5, 6, 7, 9, 12, 15, 16, 17, 20, 22, 23, 26, 30, 31, 32, 36, 37, 38, 45, 46, 49, 50, 54, 63, 68, 78, 81, 83, 91, 103.

E. J. Tallant Collection: 51.

Elinor Bluemel Collection: 97.

Fred & Jo Mazzulla Collection: 61.

Pioneer Museum Collection, Colorado Springs, Colo.: 76, 82, 93, 94.

Francis Rizzari Collection: 66.

R. A. Ronzio Collection: 28, 43, 48, 52, 57.

Charles Ryland Collection: 9, 16, 18, 19, 24, 28, 32, 35, 41, 47, 50, 51, 65, 66, 72, 74, 78, 82, 84, 86, 87, 93, 98, 102.

Jackson C. Thode Collection: 103.

ARTWORK AND SKETCHES

L. Coulson Hageman: Inside Front and Back Covers, 1, 62, 91.
Typography: Charles Ryland.
Text and Design Correlation: E.J. Tallant.

BIBLIOGRAPHY

GENERAL:

Athearn, Robert G., "High Country Empire." Lincoln, University of Nebraska Press, 1960.

Bancroft, Caroline, "Colorful Colorado, Its Dramatic History." Boulder, Johnson Publishing Company, 1959.
(Also, various other Bancroft booklets.)

Crofutt, Geo. A. "Grip-Sack Guide of Colorado" 1885. Reprint, Cubar Associates, Golden, 1966.

Dallas, Sandra, "Gaslights to Gingerbread." Denver, Sage Books, 1965.

Eberhart, Perry, "Guide to the Colorado Ghost Towns and Mining Camps." Denver, Sage Books, 1959.

Hafen, LeRoy R., "The History of Colorado." Denver, Linderman Co., Inc., 1927.

Hunt, Inez, and Wanetta W. Draper, "To Colorado's Restless Ghosts." Denver, Sage Books, 1960.

Lee, W. Storrs, "Colorado, A Literary Chronicle." New York, Funk & Wagnalls, 1970. (Selected episodes from reports and writings of various explorers and authors about Colorado.)

Ubbelohde, Carl, "A Colorado History." Boulder, Pruett Press, Inc., 1965. (A "chronological narrative from pre-historic Indians to modern missile factories.")

Wolle, Muriel S., "Stampede to Timberline." Published by Author, 1949.

Works Progress Administration, "Colorado, A Guide to the Highest State." New York, Hastings House, 1941. (Revised September 1970).

TOPICAL:

The Explorers:

Hollon, W. Eugene, "The Lost Pathfinder—Zebulon Montgomery Pike." Norman, University of Oklahoma Press, 1949.

Terrell, John Upton, "Zebulon Pike, The Life and Times of an Adventurer." New York, Weybright & Talley, Inc., 1968.

Wood, Richard G., "Stephen Harriman Long, 1784-1864, Army Engineer, Explorer, Inventor." Glendale, The Arthur H. Clark Co., 1966.

The Mountain Men:

Hafen, LeRoy R., "The Mountain Men and the Fur Trade of the Far West." Glendale, The Arthur H. Clark Company, 1969.

Lavender, David, "Bent's Fort." Garden City, N.J., Doubleday, 1954.

Estergreen, M. Morgan, "Kit Carson, A Portrait in Courage." Norman, University of Oklahoma Press, 1962.

Vestal, Stanley, "Kit Carson, The Happy Warrior of the Old West." Boston & New York, Houghton Mifflin Co., 1928.

113

Indians on the Warpath:
  Brown, Dee, "Bury My Heart At Wounded Knee." New York, Holt, Rinehart & Winston, 1970.
  Coffin, Morse H., "The Battle of Sand Creek." Waco, Texas, W. M. Morrison, 1965.
  Emmitt, Robert, "The Last War Trail." Norman, University of Oklahoma Press, 1954.
  Sprague, Marshall, "Massacre: The Tragedy at White River." Boston, Little, Brown, Inc., 1957.
Paydirt!
  McMechen, Edgar C., "Life of Governor Evans, Second Territorial Governor of Colorado." Copyright by Author, 1924.
  Ellis, Elmer, "Henry Moore Teller." Caldwell, Ida., The Caxton Printers, Ltd., 1941.
  Karsner, David, "Silver Dollar—The Story of the Tabors." New York, Covici, Friede, 1932.
  King, Otis A., "Grey Gold." Denver, Big Mountain Press, 1959.
  Wentworth, Frank L., "Aspen on the Roaring Fork." Lakewood, Colo., Francis B. Rizzari, 1950.
  Lipsey, John J., "The Lives of James John Hagerman." Denver, Golden Bell Press, 1968.
  Francis, Theresa V., "Crystal River Saga." Published by Author, 1959.
  McLean, Evalyn Walsh, "Father Struck It Rich." Boston, Little, Brown & Co., 1956.
  Hunt, Inez, and Wanetta W. Draper, "Lightning In His Hands." Denver, Sage Books, 1964.
  Fenwick, Robert W., "Alfred Packer, The True Story of the Man-Eater." Copyright by Denver Post, 1963; Printed by Publishers Press of Denver.
Sky Pilots:
  Dyer, John L., "The Snowshoe Itinerant." Published by Author, 1891; out of print.
The Empire Builders:
  McMechen, Edgar C., "The Moffat Tunnel of Colorado, An Epic of Empire." Two Volumes. Denver, Wahlgren, 1927.
  Anderson, George L., "General William J. Palmer, a Decade of Colorado Railroad Building." Colorado Springs, Colorado College Publication, 1936.
  Wilcox, Rhoda, "Man on the Iron Horse." Colorado Springs, Dentan Printing Co., 1959. (The story of General Palmer.)
  Athearn, Robert G., "Rebel of the Rockies." New Haven, Yale University Press, 1962.
The Bowl of Gold:
  Sprague, Marshall, "Money Mountain." Boston, Little, Brown & Co., 1953.
  Sprague, Marshall, "Newport in the Rockies." Denver, Sage Books, 1961.
  Waters, Frank, "Midas of the Rockies." Denver, Sage Books, 1946.